SHEPHERDING
IN THE LOCAL
CHURCH

A PROGRAM
OF PASTORAL CARE

BY JOSEPH C. GRANA II

First Printing, January, 1981

Copyright Registration Number TX-46-131

TABLE OF CONTENTS

iv

ACKNOWLEDGMENTS

I am led to thank two people who have been instrumental in assisting me. My secretary, Jan Haenel, was responsible for typing the rough draft and for drawing the logo of pastoral ministry. Her assistance is greatly appreciated.

The other person is my lovely wife, Linda. She graciously typed this final copy. Without her love and support I could not have finished this project or even effectively continued in the ministry. The debt I owe for her ministry of healing, sustaining, and guiding to me can never be repaid. I praise the "Great Shepherd" for having her shepherd me when I have gone astray.

INTRODUCTION

Since becoming a Christian in 1961 my affiliation has been with the Independent Christian Church. In this context I grew during my teen years and was challenged to the full-time leadership ministry.

My observation during this time has been the immensity of meeting the needs of a congregation. I recognized, from my perspective, that this ministry of care was impossible for one person or a small group of persons to perform. This fact appeared true to me regardless of the congregation's size. I, therefore, sought a means by which the needs of the congregation could be adequately met.

This search led me to the Bible. The image of Shepherding as describing the elders' work struck me. My thought progressed to apply this image to a group of people, under the direction of the elders, within the congregation to perform pastoral care for the entire congregation. My hope was that through such a group providing pastoral ministry, the needs of the congregation may be met.

Upon searching for Shepherding material, I was surprised with its scarcity. This fact is particularly true in regard to care by members of the congregation. Usually, I found the image of Shepherd to be applied solely to the 'pastor' of the church. I hope, therefore, that this work is a contribution to the church's ministry of caring.

The use of the concept "Shepherding" has been challenged by some to be archaic and meaningless to a technological, urban society. Therefore, it becomes initially necessary to defend and explain the use of the title, "Shepherding in the Local Congregation: A Program of Pastoral Care."

In writing about the shepherding metaphor of ministry Seward Hiltner states that culture's move from agriculture to industrial civilization need not render the metaphor irrelevant or meaningless for the basic needs that pastoral care tries to meet remain the same from age to age.[1] Samuel Calian relates,

> We have seen . . . that this particular style meets with very favorable expectation from a large number of laity. This model of ministry seeks to serve 'without acclaim', and attempts to minister with sensitivity to the needs of people individually and in groups. . . . This model is based upon Jesus as the suffering servant. . . . There is no doubt that the practice of this model of ministry is deeply satisfying.[2]

In spite of these positive statements it is necessary to analyze this image. The sheep should be understood as representing need, not stupidity or innocence. Each sheep is important. The shepherd does not know everything. He is a fellow struggler. The image, therefore, deals with concerns and attitudes, not methods and procedures. The aim of shepherding is to help the person to move as far in the direction of healing as circumstances permit.

By looking at the drawing on the next page one sees these concerns. When the need is present, the shepherd meets it. He removes the burr, but does not moralize to the sheep about having run off course. The sheep is respected for the shepherd may be the next to be needing help. Having walked through the rough terrain with many thorns shows that the shepherd experiences the same dangers as the sheep. By kneeling he shows that there is no difference in

2

status. The attitude is one of humility.[4] In the third sketch the shepherd brings the straying sheep back into the fold. The goals of shepherding involve individual healing and care, but also community concerns.

The Scriptures continually picture shepherds as participants in the activities into which they lead their sheep. They are not armchair theorists, but rather down there on the plain, up there in the mountains, traveling the paths trod by the sheep themselves. Their leadership is concrete, participative and involved. Shepherds are with the sheep. They keep watch over their flocks by night, pass through the valleys where in every shadow lurks the possibility of death from a wild animal and gently lead those with young (Isaiah 40:11; Ezekiel 34:15; Psalm 23). The shepherd "leads them out" of the fold and "goes before them" (John 10:3,4). He defends them from the wolf with his rod. The shepherd is an involved example.[5]

As the image of shepherding originates from the agrarian situation where a man took a flock by day to protect and watch them, so the Christian metaphor refers to the tender and individual care by the shepherd for the sheep. Healing is the aim although it is not always possible. This healing involves all levels of the person.[6] Healing may occur physically, mentally (emotionally), socially, and spiritually. This author's opinion is that this metaphor is understandable and relevant to the Christian community because of its wide use in Scripture. Furthermore, it seems to be uniquely Christian in that Christ is called the "Great Shepherd." When shepherding is seen as healing, sustaining, and guiding as Hiltner demonstrates, the image may well come alive for the Twentieth Century Church.

A problem with this image is that the term "Pastor" has been equated with "Minister" and, therefore, implies that the shepherding is done by this individual. Calian declares,

> Actually the servant-shepherd model should include all persons who consider themselves among the people of God. In other words, this model is not exclusively limited to the professional clergy. The servant-shepherd model applies to the entire *laos* - the people of God. . . . We have **all** been baptized into a common priesthood. There are no first and second class Christians.[7]

What the church most needs today is wise shepherding that senses the true nature of the longings, the fears, the troubles, and the acute needs of the flock. Creative shepherding will lead to guiding the flock to greener pastures and beside still waters.[8] This program is addressed to that concept. No image or program of pastoral care is one hundred per cent effective, but the program is designed to bring healing to congregations. It would be ideal if every member of the church was so filled with the love of Christ that he had an automatic concern for his fellow members. The experience of many, however, confirms that many noble resolves soon die away unless there is some built-in development for nudging the will to action.[9] This fact demonstrates the justification of such a program. Jay Adams agrees **when** he writes that **when** adequate fellowship is built into congregational activity (and today it must be **built in** consciously since it no longer comes naturally in these urbanized times in which we live), the church will not complain about the structure nor will there be serious questions about preaching and teaching.[10]

Shepherding advocates service. "The church's task in the secular city is to be the *Diakonos* of the city, the servant who bends himself to struggle for its wholeness and health."[11] Hopefully, shepherding is a step towards such wholeness and health within the church and community.

The church is the church only as it exists for others.[12] Avery Dulles explains that the church proclaims the Kingdom through the ministry of reconciliation and by binding wounds, suffering service, and healing. The shepherding metaphor, therefore, exemplifies that kind of servanthood that could make the world declare, "See how they love one another!" The Church's mission, in the perspectives of this shepherding theology, is not primarily to gain new recruits for its own ranks but rather to be of help to all men, wherever they are,[13] especially within the community of faith.

The participation of many within the congregation is necessary to make this theology a reality. The "laymen" are the key as they perform acts of healing for one another. The undergirding foundation and premise of shepherding is the priesthood of **all** believers. This premise is a reminder to all Christians that their time, talents, and resources are on loan to them from God. Each Christian is called into a priestly vocation.[14] If the members of the congregation are not convinced of the necessity of healing through shepherding, the program will not effectively work.

In talking about the many contributions of the people in the parish, Cornelius Holland writes,

> In view of all this tremendous contribution to the life of a parish indeed, could parishes go on without it? - How great should be the pastor's interest in it and how great should be his appreciation of, and his gratitude to, those who provide it.[15]

The joy of shepherding is felt by pastor, shepherd, and flock. Healing comes to all involved when real care and love are shown. An anonymous poet put it well:

I went to see a sick friend
For years he'd been in bed;
I thought to cheer him up a bit,
but he cheered me instead.

My aim, therefore, will be to depict the Shepherding Program as developed at the Central Christian Church in Beloit, Wisconsin. I will deal with the shepherding theological rationale in chapter one; needs for the problems of shepherding in chapter two; the organization of the program in chapter three; the responsibility, enlistment, and training of shepherds in chapter four; evaluation of the program in chapter five; and conclusions and future possibilities in chapter six.

NOTES

[1]Seward Hiltner, *Ferment in the Ministry* (New York: Abingdon Press, 1969), p. 106.

[2]Carnegie Samuel Calian, *Today's Pastor in Tomorrow's World* (New York: Hawthorn Books, 1977), p. 9.

[3]Seward Hiltner, *The Christian Shepherd* (New York: Abingdon Press, 1959), pp. 19, 20.

[4]Idem, *Ferment in Ministry* (New York: Abingdon Press, 1969), p. 106.

[5]Jay Adams, *Pastoral Leadership* (Grand Rapids: Baker Book House, 1975), pp. 6, 7.

[6]Hiltner, *The Christian Shepherd*, pp. 20, 21.

[7]Calian, *Today's Pastor in Tomorrow's World*, p. 10.

[8]Jay Adams, *The Pastoral Life* (Grand Rapids: Baker Book House, 1974), p. 79.

[9]Charlie Shedd, *The Pastoral Ministry of Church Officers* (Atlanta: John Knox Press, 1977), p. 18.

[10]Adams, *The Pastoral Life*, p. 79.

[11]Harvey Cox, *The Secular City* (New York: Macmillan, 1965), p. 134.

[12]Avery Dulles, *Models of the Church* (Garden City: New York: Doubleday, 1974), p. 88.

[13]*Ibid.*, p. 91.

[14]Calian, *Today's Pastor in Tomorrow's World*, p. 11.

[15]Cornelius Joseph Holland, *The Shepherd and His Flock* (New York: David McKay Co., 1053), p. 72.

CHAPTER 1

Biblical and Theological Foundations for Shepherding

Delight in Teaching What You Have Learned.
Seneca

SIGNIFICANT WORDS

The Scriptures were created out of human experience with the Divine. The directions of God's will and the wisdom of men led by the Holy Spirit resulted in the written Word which is "profitable for teaching, for reproof, for correction, and for training in righteousness" (II Timothy 3:16). These men of God were delighted to teach what they learned. This knowledge is applicable today and this author delights in the opportunity to teach what he has learned from those who taught what they have learned. My judgment and presupposition is that any justification for a program by a church must have a foundation which is biblically based. The purpose of this chapter is to briefly expose those passages which justify and give direction to "A Shepherding Program of Pastoral Care."

In construction it is necessary to secure a firm footing for a building, so is it in developing a concept of theology. The Shepherding Model of Ministry for a total congregation begins with the footing of the "Priesthood of Believers." To understand this thesis it is necessary to briefly make some word studies of significant terms.

The term "priest" is not applied to any particular class of persons within the Christian community, though the entire Christian community is designated as a "priestly people."[1] The term "priesthood" is only found in I Peter 2:5,9 in the New Testament and Exodus 19:6 and 23:22 in the Septuagint. Vine states that this word denotes a priesthood or a body of priests, consisting of all believers: the whole church.[2] This priesthood results in a ministry of witness to all humanity (as in Isaiah 61:6).[3]

A subsequent study of these Scriptures will assist in demonstrating the role of the complete congregation in performing priestly functions. Unmistakenly, the term "priest" as used in the New Testament does not refer to officiants in a church building but describes all Christians in their role as the priesthood of all believers.[4] Biblically speaking there are three priesthoods:

1. Levitical (Hebrew - *Kohen*)
2. Christ (Greek - *Hierus*, which translates *Kohen* in the Septuagint). Hebrews 7:12
3. Church (Greek - *Hierateuma* and *Hierateia*). Isaiah 61:6; Exodus 19:5,6; I Peter 2:9,10; Revelation 1:6, 5:10

I have observed a hermeneutic by New Testament writers in reference to Old Testament passages that interpret the Old Testament as fulfilled in Christ and the Church. For instance, the Temple of the Old Testament (*Naos*, Holy of Holies) is seen as fulfilled in the church (I Corinthians 3:16). Other practices such as sacrifices, circumcision, the Passover Feast and even the nation of Israel were shadows of what was to come with the establishment of the church. The priesthood in like manner was intended for the whole church. As the priests offered physical sacrifices, so the entire Christian community is called to offer spiritual sacrifices consisting of holy lives. Christians are to offer themselves, their souls and bodies to God in witness to Christ before the non-Christian world.[5]

Another important and interesting word is "clergy." This term is derived from *Kleros* which literally means "A part of a share." *Kleros* is found in Acts 1:17 in discussing the vacated Apostolic office of Judas. Donald Nash explains that the Apostles were a "clergy" of the church, a distinct part of the ministry of Christ's Kingdom, but they were not the only part. There is a Scriptural clergy of apostles, prophets, evangelists, pastors-teachers, elders, deacons. However, every member has a part (clergy) in the body according to I Corinthians 12:1ff.[6] Oscar Feucht makes these comments about the term "clergy":

> The word "clergy" is derived from the Greek word *kleros*. It originally meant the object used in drawing lots to choose a person for a position. It is related to the verb "call" and is employed in the Greek New Testament when referring to the Holy Spirit calling a person by the Gospel into the Christian fellowship of the church. We can understand its meaning better if we see how it is used: "Called to be God's people. . . . When God called you. . . . To which God has called you" (Ephesians 4:1,4 TEV); "He saved us and called us to be His own people" (II Timothy 1:9 TEV).
>
> In each of these verses some form of the Greek word "to call" is used. All Christians are God's called people, God's "clergy" in the world! Even the Greek word for the church, *ekklesia*, is derived from the basic term "to call."[7]

Nash explains that the error of the so-called "clergy system" is that special authority was historically given by denominations to preachers (or priests) when in reality the New Testament teaches the priesthood of all believers (I Peter 2:9; Revelation 1:6). Authority in the church resides primarily in Christ the Head (Colossians 1:18); secondarily in Apostles, to whom authority was given to reveal

Christ's will (Ephesians 2:20); and in the local congregation to elders (Acts 20:28).[8] There is a need for the "clergy" of preachers, but also the "clergy" of the rest of the church. There are not to be classes of Christians in Christ's church, just different functions (parts) to perform.[9]

OLD TESTAMENT

In Exodus 19:6 God instructs Moses to tell Israel, "You shall be to me a Kingdom of priests and a Holy Nation."[10] Cyril Eastwood comments that Israel was to learn the important lessons that they were recipients of a revelation of grace, that it was a revelation to the whole of Israel, and that it could be forfeited by disobedience and self-will.[11] The second lesson espoused by Eastwood is the point of this discussion. As a member of a priestly people, ideally no Israelite had any privileges over another in drawing near and presenting offerings to Jehovah. Throughout the history of Israel this privilege was for the most part taken advantage of, and any Israelite felt entitled to offer sacrifices to the Lord. E. Best lists Scriptures which relate the spiritual sacrifices which every Israelite should offer (Isaiah 1:11-15; Hosea 6:6; Micah 6:6-8; Psalms 50:13,14,23; 51:17; 141:2).[12]

Leviticus 26:12, which is also restated in Jeremiah 11:4, declares, "You shall be my people." Jeremiah wisely observed that the history of the Hebrews from the Egyptian Exodus to his own day was simply the realization of that promise.[13] As a priestly nation, all the people had direct access to God. Again, Revelation 21:3 views the church in this same light.

Apparently, the concept of community responsibility in priesthood was emphasized in the people Moses led. In Numbers 16:3 Moses is

12

confronted with, "You have gone too far! For all the congregation are holy, every one of them; why then do you exalt yourselves about the assembly of the Lord?" Moses was challenged on his inconsistencies (from the complainers' viewpoint) concerning a Kingdom of Priests. Eastwood believes three truths stand out clearly in Jewish teaching on this subject:

    a. The priestly prerogative of the whole community (Numbers 11:29)

    b. The priestly duties of the whole community

    Three demands were made of Jews in general

      1. Learned in the law

      2. Minister in the sanctuary of the spiritual

      3. Devote their minds and hearts to doctrine of the Jewish faith.

    c. Individual responsibility of each member for the spiritual welfare of the whole community.[14]

The church as the fulfillment of Israel has the same responsibilities.

NEW TESTAMENT

One of the most striking aspects of primitive Christianity was the almost total eclipse of the priestly role of Old Testament religion. Very early Christians began to use the word "minister" which is the equivalent of "servant." However, nowhere in the New Testament or in other early Christian literature is the word *Hierus*, "priest," employed as the equivalent of the Christian ministry.[15] As has been briefly demonstrated, the essence of the matter is to be found in the Old Testament idea of the children of Israel. Priests, prophets, and people are all together the people of God. This idea is taken over and developed in the New Testament, particularly by Paul, as the "church."[16] The death knell to a special system of priests with a favored position before God was symbolized when Jesus was hanged on the cross and the great curtain in the temple which separated the Holy Place from the Holy of Holies was ripped in two (Luke 23:45). The Holy of Holies became available to any believer, not just the High Priest. In the New Covenant all of God's people are to be "a royal priesthood" (I Peter 2:9) with Jesus Christ functioning as the new High Priest (Hebrews 4:14).[17]

In my opinion, the most outstanding New Testament passage in reference to the priesthood of believers and the one most closely associated to the Old Testament verses discussed is I Peter 2:4-10. No less than six titles are assigned to the Christian in these verses. The titles are based on Old Testament promises and figures of speech. By using Old Testament words and phrases in place of his own, Peter is giving to his own arguments that authority which he allowed the Old Testament to possess.[18] According to this catalogue of titles, every Christian is:

    (1)   Claimed by God
    (2)   Belongs to a Holy Nation
    (3)   Set apart for a particular ministry
    (4)   To fulfill in his life both a kingship and a priesthood.

I believe there is great significance in noting that these are the words of the Apostle Peter, one of the three disciples closest to our Lord. These titles raise all believers to the status of "ministers."[19] If anyone was in the position to propagate classes and distinctions between Christians, it was Peter. However, he chose not to do so because this was not

God's plan.

Best is convinced that Peter's mind as revealed in this Epistle is not creative. He believes it unlikely that Peter derived from Exodus 19:6 the concept of the priesthood of the church. More likely is that Peter knew the tradition of the primitive church and then applied Exodus 19:6 to it.[20] Best continues his study by pointing out that upon a careful examination of words ending in *Euma*, one will discover that these words indicate a community of persons functioning in a particular capacity. This fact is further attested in 2:9, in Best's opinion, by the phrase *Basileion Hiereuma* (commonly translated "Royal Priesthood"). Peter usually places his adjectives after the noun they qualify.[21] Therefore, this phrase would be understood as a priesthood or "Body of Kings." The idea expressed is one of corporate responsibility and privilege.

God chose men like Abraham, Moses, and Joshua to lead His people. Jeremiah writes of a new age for all the people of God. "I (God) will put my law within them, and I will write it upon their hearts, and I will be their God, and they shall be my people" (Jeremiah 31:31-33). The book of Hebrews indicates that the Old Covenant system was temporary until all of God's people would form the priesthood of the New Covenent (Hebrews 8:8,10).[22]

The church, in my opinion, is the fulfillment of that concept and prophecy. Luther believed that Christians are *Allesampt durch die tauff zu priesten geweht* ("All ordained as priests through baptism").[23] One enters the church through faith and baptism and, therefore, also priesthood. Zwingli agreed that we are all fully ordained to the priesthood, but we are not all Apostles and Bishops.[24] In other words, all Christians are clergy, but there is also a need for leadership roles.

In I Peter 2:5 the figure of speech changes. The believers are priests offering themselves to God in daily service in all that they do, are, and say. Verses six and eight are quotations from Isaiah 8:14. Their use indicates that the rejection of Jesus, His suffering, death, and resurrection were all part of God's great plan for salvation predicted by the Old Testament prophets. Christ became the cornerstone of the church. All believers have become living stones built into that Temple. The Holy Spirit is the Architect. The Christians, therefore, are building blocks.[25]

Verse nine reaffirms this position of the church, but also adds some of the duties or expectations. God's people are to offer spirit-motivated sacrifices (2:5) and to proclaim publicly God's mighty saving deeds. What is involved in these? The previous context of 1:3; 2:3 tells us the stress is primarily upon the leading of a life of holy obedience to the will of God (1:14-18,22; 2:1), a holy life tempered with the hope and joy (1:3-8), alertness (1:13), and brotherly love (1:22; 2:1).[26]

In verses nine and ten the term *Laos* (laity, people) is used quite extensively. A study of the word "laity" reveals that it is derived from the Greek word *Laos* which means "people," usually God's chosen people: Christians. From *Laos* we get the word "layman." The term "layman" today means someone who is an amateur, one who does not understand. That concept does not coincide with the scriptural definition of "layman" as demonstrated in these verses. Mark Gibbs and T. Ralph Norton have written a book entitled, *God's Frozen People*, which is designed to abolish the Christian layman (as understood today) and to make Christians experts instead. The whole church is "clergy" and, therefore, should have expertise in ministry according to the gifts God has bestowed. The Shepherd Program is a step in creating that reality.

Although the I Peter passage is the main pericope of the Priesthood of Believer Doctrine, other Scriptures also indicate it. I Corinthians 12 develops the thought of universal priesthood, while never using the term. Verses four and eleven demonstrate that a variety of gifts are distributed by the Holy Spirit to various members of the church. In verses twelve to twenty-six Paul explains that the purpose of the various gifts is for mutual service because the many members are part of one body. Eight gifts are listed in verses twenty-seven through thirty-one to assist the body towards independence and unity. Those possessing these gifts were not officials but functionaries of the church. Paul develops the analogy of the body in this passage to teach us about our relationship with each other. Believers are dependent on each other. God has called us to a community of faith and service. No one person is fully equipped with all the spiritual gifts. Instead, each Christian is given his own distinctive gift or gifts. Each "priest" makes his own unique contribution to the common good.[27] The church is to develop interrelationships and mutual helpfulness so as to be cooperative and complementary like the members and organs of the human body.

During the early days of the church, "ministry" referred to all the services rendered by the Christian community, regardless of who rendered them. Most probably these actual ministries were complex.[28] When Paul tells the Corinthians to preserve good order, he makes no mention of local authoritative leaders whom they should obey. In fact, there is a strong case for concluding that there were then no officeholders in the Church of Corinth. The early church's ministry became indigenous. The Apostles and other prominent missionaries left behind them a ministry of local men.[29]

The direction of the above thought certainly coincides with the Doctrine of the Priesthood of Believers. Every member of the body has a priestly function according to his gift. The necessity within the church is, therefore, unity and mutuality. As no one person possesses all the spiritual gifts, so no one person or small group of persons can perform a ministry which effectively meets the total needs of the whole church. If a congregation takes the preceding idea of ministry seriously, the result will not be a congregation with a minister, but, rather, a ministering congregation. Congregational participation in ministry is not simply sitting in a prescribed number of worship services. A ministering-congregation eliminates the concept of three hundred members with one minister, but now has ideally three hundred ministers.[30]

This Priesthood of All Believers is based upon the fact that all believers share a common dignity. It is not true that some Christians belong to a religious class and others do not. The honor and dignity conferred by Christ upon one is also conferred upon any believer.[31] There is one Baptism, one Gospel, and one Faith, and all are equally Christian. The functions of each Christian are different, but each is able to have the same relationship to the Head, Christ. The concept that the clergy are closer or more special to God than the layman is erroneous, for all Christians are to be clergy and laymen. On this basis all Christians have the same call, but different avenues of services.[32]

CHURCH HISTORY:
FATHERS AND DENOMINATIONS

The church has historically revered the teaching and opinions of the Church Fathers and other great men of God. Although I do not place any authority in these men, I recognize that wisdom can be solicited from their counsel. Their influence has made an impact upon Christendom and, therefore, they deserve at least a brief perusal. Their statements will assist in confirming the views presented from the Biblical material. However, I understand that not all totally agree with this precept.

Cyril Eastwood in his book *The Royal Priesthood of the Faithful* on pages fifty-six through eighty summarizes the views of several early Church Fathers concerning this teaching. These men and their thoughts are succinctly listed as presented by Eastwood:

Clement (1st Century)	The Laity can baptize, take deathbed confessions, and preach. The congregation is the supreme authority.
Polycarp (70-156)	Discipline is by the authority of the congregation. Through the Priesthood of Christ all Christians are given a part in the life and work of the church, women are included in the Priesthood of all Believers, and all members are called upon to exercise this priesthood in questions of discipline.
Justin Martyr (100-165)	We are not only a people, but a Holy people.
Iaenaeus (125-202)	The church has a priestly character.

Clement of Alexandria (150-216)	Those receiving the *Gnosis* direct from the Master and are obedient to His commands are the "true priests".
Tertullian (155-222)	The main authority and responsibility rests with the clergy.
Origen (185-254)	Christians reveal their true priesthood in holiness of character, in the sacrifices they offer in worship, and in the readiness to hold confessions even in face of martyrdom.[33]

The attitude and practice of the Church changed, however, and the structure and mechanics of the church evolved into another pattern. During Constantine's reign a hierarchical system of leadership developed in the church. This system was patterned after the political system.[34] This change developed a clergy-dominated church, with little expected from the peasants except obedience.[35] The Priesthood of Believers was not extinct but for the most part dormant until the Reformation. The Reformation fostered the revival of the scriptural principles previously mentioned. A look at some of these leaders is in order.

Luther

The most renowned reformer in my opinion is Martin Luther[36] who viewed the ministry as placed in the hands of the congregation.[37] He was convinced that all believers share a common dignity, calling, and privilege. He believed the power to ordain those who are set aside for the work of the ministry is within the province of the whole church. A person is not "made" a minister merely by an act of orderly vocation from the congregation nor by performing some occasional priestly acts. On the contrary, one's membership in the Royal Priesthood enables him to exercise priestly functions.[38]

Historically, however, the renewal of interest in lay participation was short-lived in the German church. This fact also became true in other European countries, and the Priesthood of Believers was soon relegated to a minor role.[39] In spite of this fact, one views from church history a remnant that continued to believe in a "laity priesthood." With the voice of strong leadership this teaching continued to be sounded forth even though its practice may not have been universally manifested.

Calvin:

Calvin's theology viewed the Priesthood of all Believers not in some obscure manner but as a main doctrine. Calvine expressed the Universal Priesthood in the worship, intercession, witness, and service of the whole community.[40]

Calvin explicitly believed that even though all are polluted, in Christ all became priests. Therefore, every believer should offer himself and his all to God.[41] This statement by John Calvin combined with the above investigation supports the scriptural views stated: the whole church is full of priests.

The historical statements about the Priesthood of Believers are immense. More statements from the Church Fathers and various denominations are available. At the end of this work, views of some denominations or people within the denominations are shared to demonstrate the widespread acceptance of this doctrine. These statements are not exhaustive but merely representative of the historical view of priesthood.

Hopefully, one can see that the concept of the Priesthood of Believers has been of great significance to Christendom.[42] This foundation of necessity must be secure before shepherding as depicted in this work can be understood and accepted. Shepherding, in my opinion, is the responsibility and privilege of the total church, not just the paid clergy. Christ, our High Priest, has made all Christians-Priests unto God. From this premise, it is now possible to view a theology of shepherding.

A THEOLOGY OF SHEPHERDING

Shepherding from the Biblical period to our own day is unique to Christianity. Other religions have spiritual directors who minister with people as individuals or in small groups. The concept of dealing with people in terms of shepherding, which looks toward healing in a holistic sense, however, is unique to Christianity and Judaism.[43] The uniqueness of the approach given in this treatise is that the whole church is seen in terms of shepherding one another. Too often this role has been left for "the pastor." His title in itself tends to focus this responsibility upon him. Certainly, he is to shepherd the flock as Seward Hiltner, Jay Adams, and others have demonstrated, but he is not "the shepherd." To call the Christians who fulfill this responsibility "under shepherds" is a misnomer in my opinion. While all Christians are under Christ, all Christians are on an equal plane. Jesus was sent by God yet called the twelve Apostles, not under-Apostles, because they were under His authority. When the church, the priesthood of all believers, views themselves as shepherds, then healing, sustaining, and guiding will be a vital function of the Body of Christ.

The term "Shepherd" (*Poimen*) is found sparingly in the New Testament. W.E. Vine demonstrates its usage in the following manner:

(1) In its natural significance
Matthew 9:36; 26:32; Mark 6:34; Luke 2:8,15,18,20; John 10:2,12.

(2) Metaphorically of Christ
   Matthew 26:31; Mark 14:27, John 10:11,14,16; Hebrews 13:20;
   I Peter 2:25.

(3) Metaphorically of those who act as pastors
   Ephesians 4:11[44]; Acts 20:28 with which verse 17 indicates that
   this was the service committed to elders . . . so also I Peter
   5:1,2.[45] [46]

The Lord is viewed in terms of a Shepherd in some very significant Scriptures which help formulate a theology of Shepherding. Probably the most well-known and beloved Scripture is Psalm 23 which not only is the image of a Shepherd portrayed, but a model of actions appropriate to Shepherds is depicted. The image begins in the first verse; "The Lord is My Shepherd."[47] As demonstrated from Hiltner's writings a Shepherd, here God, heals, sustains, and guides. These helps are necessary because sheep (ourselves) are far often helpless (Isaiah 53:7), followers (John 10:3-5), and wander (Isaiah 53:6).

Jay Adams[48] has analyzed this Psalm in terms of Shepherding and points out the following performances that this Scripture depicts a Shepherd doing. Though this activity is credited to God's healing with man, there seems to be no reason, in my opinion, why this example cannot be applied to fellow Christians.

(1) Concern for each individual sheep
   Individual concern is understood by the use of "My Shepherd." The personal pronoun focuses the attention specifically. Statements by Jesus confirm this thought. In John 10:3 He says, "He calls His own sheep by name." Again in John 10:27 "My sheep hear my voice, and I know them, and they follow me." Luke 15:4 explains the parable of the Shepherd who leaves the ninety-nine to seek one lost sheep. God's concern is for individuals who are known personally

and whose individual needs are considered and met. Without personal attention one's dignity and significance are often questioned. God does not leave mankind, who is made in His image, in this dilemma.

(2) Rest

The Psalmist states, "He makes me lie down." The Shepherd, due to his personal relationship knows what is too much for his flock. Adequate rest (Psalm 127:2) is needed to function properly and for healing. The concerned Shepherd guides those under his care to a rest which will sustain them.

(3) Provisions for Daily Sustenance

". . . in green pastures. He leads me beside still waters" (23:2). This image shows a concern for food and drink. God is portrayed throughout the Scriptures as fulfilling the physical needs of His children (Matthew 6:25-33). The model prayer (Matthew 6:9-13) petitions for daily bread. The church, likewise, is encouraged to take care of the necessities of its members (Acts 6:1-7; Galatians 6:2; James 2:14-17). Jesus performed a vital ministry besides manifesting miraculous powers when he fed the multitudes.

(4) Refreshment and Encouragement

"He restores my soul" (23:3). Francis MacNutt in his book *Healing* lists four kinds of healing for people: forgiveness of sin (through repentance), inner healing of emotional problems, physical healing, and deliverance (from demons).[49] This aspect of Shepherding would more closely relate to inner healing. MacNutt sees this healing as overcoming memories. The inner man is healed when one's soul is freed from past hurts. God provides encouragement for these times, and his ministers (Shepherds) can perform the same ministry.

(5) Guidance and Leadership)

"He leads me" (23:3). A note of great significance here is that the Lord leads - He does not drive or push. Other Scriptures stating the same thought are Psalm 80:1; John 10:3,4; Revelation 7:17. By guiding, the Lord provides leadership which facilitates healing. Human dignity is enhanced through responsibility. When led, people may follow voluntarily, but when driven, the choice, and therefore, the reward are often nullified.

(6) Instruction, Training, and Discipline

"He leads me in paths of righteousness" (23:3). The guidance and the following are not mindless. God has given the Scriptures which are profitable for teaching, for reproof, for correction, and for training in righteousness (II Timothy 3:16). God's inspired Word disciplines one to know and walk the paths of righteousness. Its timeless truths are still effective for this purpose.

(7) Provisions for Goals and Motivation

"For His name's sake" (23:3). After trying everything he believed the world could offer in happiness and motivation, the writer of Ecclesiastes concludes, "Fear God, and keep His commandments; for this is the whole duty of man" (12:13). Man needs to be drawn to God. Jesus said, "And I, when I am lifted up from the earth, will draw all men to myself" (John 12:32). Likewise, the motivation and goal of a Shepherd is for God's sake and glory.

(8) Security and Protection

"I will fear no evil" (23:4). The assurance of God's presence, guiding, healing, and sustaining gives one security. As the hymn goes, "God will take care of you." To realize that another human being is willing to do the above Shepherding can also provide security and protection. The expression of brotherly concern through action and the explanation of God's concern through instruction can greatly help a wandering soul.

(9) Personal Fellowship and Loving Friendship

"Thou art with me" (23:4). Man is a social being. Personal relationships are very meaningful to most people. Christianity is a faith based on relationships. God does not call Christians to rules and regulations, but to a vital relationship with a Risen Savior. Furthermore, one's call into the church is not one just for corporate ritual but a call into a community of relationships. What the world needs now is love, God's love. The Great Shepherd through his priesthood of believers can provide for that vital need of man.[51]

By briefly looking at the twenty-third Psalm one can catch a glimpse of what Shepherding involves. As God is that type of Shepherd,[52] so should his people emulate that type of behavior. The correlation between this image and theology of Shepherding and its practical application will be discussed in a later chapter.

In the New Testament the image of Shepherd is applied to Christ. This fact is particularly exhibited in the Gospel of Matthew. Martin Francis[53], in a study of the passages, notes that healing is the primary motif of Christ's Shepherding. A brief summary of this thoughts with comments by myself will be offered.

The first reference is Matthew 2:6. This Scripture is a quote from Micah 5:1 and II Samuel 5:2. The word translated "rule" or "govern" is actually the verb *poimen*, "to Shepherd." Christ came to guide, to sustain, and to heal God's people Israel. It is interesting to note that this image was given to Jesus as one who came from Bethlehem, the City of David, who was himself a Shepherd.

In Matthew 9:36 Jesus sees the people as sheep without a Shepherd and in 10:6 He sends the twelve to the lost sheep of Israel. These two verses hinge together the activity of the Disciples with the compassion of Christ. Christ's love is enacted through his people. An allusion to this pericope is found in Ezekiel 34. In this chapter God's people are scattered and disorganized, while God's Shepherds are to guide and heal them (which they do not do). The whole tone of Ezekiel 34 sees the Shepherd as a healer. This is confirmed by the Septuagint rendering of Zechariah 10:2 where we find once again the image of a scattered flock. The use of *Iasis* ("healing," literally, "doctoring") in the Septuagint reflects the use of the notion of healing as a spiritual reality.[54] Christ and His Apostles are, therefore, correctly to be viewed as, Shepherds who heal.

Christ refers to a Shepherd and his sheep in Matthew 12:9-14. The occasion for his comment is the healing of a man with a withered hand. Jesus makes an analogy between this man and a lost sheep. This image depicts a lost sheep who is rescued. The action is described by the verbs *kratein* (lay hold of) and *egerein* (raise). In other places these verbs are used to portray healing.[55] [56]

Matthew 18:12-14 portrays the Disciples as Shepherds. As leaders they must go in search of a little one who wanders.[57] The Shepherd leaves the ninety-nine for the lost one. So the Disciples, and today's Shepherds, are to care for the seemingly most insignificant person. Guidance and healing of the inner person are very significant here.

The passages concerning Christ's second coming conclude this imagery. The combination of Matthew 24:30 and 25:32 sees Christ exercising his shepherding authority at the judgment. He will separate the sheep from the goats. These passages utilize the idea of a Shepherd-King found in Deuteronomy and Zechariah. Jesus is the Shepherd-King who heals and guides.

It is significant that Matthew was writing to the Jews to demonstrate that Jesus was the fulfillment of the Old Testament prophecies. Therefore, as God is seen as the Shepherd in Psalm 23 so Christ is the fulfillment of that image. As Jesus performed his ministry of Shepherding through healing[58], so may the followers of His example. Christians are to imitate (mimic) Christ (I Corinthians 11:1; Ephesians 5:1). Therefore, today's Shepherds are to heal: body, mind, and spirit.

The parable of the Good Samaritan (Luke 10:30-35), though never mentioning the term Shepherd, demonstrates the attitude of healing previously described. The Samaritan saw human suffering and need, was sensitive to it, and did what was needed to alleviate the suffering. The Samaritan apparently loved the wounded man. Christians are also called upon to love all men as neighbors, loving each as himself. This parable demonstrates that followers are to love all true Christian brothers in a way that the world may observe. By using a Samaritan, Jesus taught men to love their brothers in the midst of differences, great or small. Love may cost something. Love may come under times of tremendous emotional tension but such a love the world can see. Love and the unity it attests to are the marks Christ gave Christians to wear before the world. Only these marks communicate to the world that Christians are indeed Christians and that Jesus was sent by the Father.[59]

This parable is but an example of what Shepherding does when a need arises. Christians are to perform a healing service as intelligently as possible under the circumstances. In this parable the Samaritan needed oil, wine, bandages, and an inn. Another occasion will necessitate a verbal testimony. This story implies that anything hindering the best possible meeting of the need for healing should be eliminated.[60]

God, therefore, has called all Christians into a ministry of Shepherding to one another. Although the program girded by these Scriptures is designed to specify certain people as Shepherds, it is the ultimate goal of this endeavor to enlighten, exhort, and encourage each Christian to be a Shepherd in his daily life. One may not possess the office, but he can still perform the function.

Another perspective of Shepherding is seen in Mark 3:14-15. In these verses Jesus appointed the twelve as Apostles and gave them authority to preach and cast out demons. Both of these activities are ways of presenting the gospel to the needs of men. Flexibility is desirable in bringing what is absolutely needed to the hearts and minds of men. Different methods are helpful when one takes into account different situations, occasions, times, and needs. Preaching and healing are ways of combining the eternal gospel with specific needs.[61]

Jesus was concerned about persons. The lack of this concern displayed may explain why people leave the church. Jesus looked to a person's inner being not his outward appearance. The Jews saw a tax-collector; Jesus saw Matthew. Society saw a woman of soiled reputation; Christ saw Mary Magdalene.[62] Jesus saw people made in the image of God. He saw what persons could be if healed, guided, and sustained. Christ did more than perceive those facts; he acted to assist in their becoming a reality.

The Theology of Shepherding is not confined to

an agrarian life-style but to the active care of the church to nurture people in Christ. The biblical expression of this ministry is only limited by the passages illuminating Christian (pastoral) care attempting healing, guiding, and sustaining. A few Scriptures which demonstrate this theology in practice are:

John 10:11-18	"I am the Good Shepherd." (We are to follow Jesus' example)
Hebrews 13:20	"Lord Jesus, that Great Shepherd of the Sheep."
John 21:15-19	Jesus said to Peter, "Feed my Sheep."[63]
Acts 20:17-35	Eldership seen as pastoring the flock.
Galatians 6:2	"Bear one another's burdens."
Acts 6:1	"Daily distribution of the food."
James 5:16	"Confess your sins to one another."
Romans 12:10	"Be devoted to one another in brotherly love."
Galatians 6:10	"Do good unto all men' but especially unto those of the household of faith."
James 2:14-17	"Faith without works is dead."

Ephesians 2:19-22	"You are fellow citizens and members of the household of God."
James 1:27	"Religion pure and undefiled is to visit orphans and widows in their afflictions."
Romans 12:13	"Contribute to the needs of the saints, practice hospitality."[64]
Ephesians 4:1	"Bearing with one another in love."
Romans 12:15	"Rejoice with those who rejoice, weep with those who weep."
James 1:19	"Be quick to listen."
Galatians 6:1	"If any man is overtaken in any trespass, you who are spiritual should restore him in a spirit of gentleness."
John 13:34	"Love one another."
Ephesians 4:2	"Help the unity of the Spirit through the bond of peace."
Matthew 7:12	"Do unto others as you would have them do unto you."

| Acts 2:42 | "And they devoted themselves to . . . fellowship." |
| Matthew 25:31-46 | "Feed the hungry, give drink to the thirsty, invite the stranger, visit the sick and those in prison." |

The last passage is of significant importance for it involves the final judgment. Christ has an expectation for his followers to care for people in need. This care and ministry has been summed up in a Theology of Shepherding. When the church fulfills this ministry as a Priesthood of Believers, it will be nearing the concept of the New Testament Church.

CONCLUSIONS

The New Testament church was marked by a genuine ministry of the laity. A thread throughout the New Testament weaves a clear call to the pastoral ministry to those who called themselves followers of Christ.[65] The priesthood of believers is essential to a Shepherding program for every Christian is or can be a Shepherd or pastor, not just the professional clergy. This biblical knowledge can encourage each and every Christian to perform healing, guiding, sustaining. Whosoever will may show compassion and do something about human needs.[66] "By this shall men know that you are my disciples, if you have love one to another . . . support the weak . . . visit the fatherless and widows . . . be kindly affectioned one toward another . . . remember the poor . . . feed the flock . . . bear one another's burdens . . . lift up the hands which hang down . . . strengthen the brethren . . . remember them that are in bonds . . . as every man has received a gift, even so minister the same one to another." Shepherding attempts to do these things.

A good summary of this chapter is set forth by Hans Kung where he describes the Christian community with three terms:

(1) Liberty - Christians are liberated by Christ from the letter of the law, the burden of guilt, the dread of death. They are at the same time, however, liberated for **life, service** and love.

(2) Equality - All members of the church have the same rights and the same duties. No one in the church has a right to abolish this fundamental equality of the faithful.

(3) Fraternity - The church is a community of brothers and sisters. They have one message and one mission - directed to all mankind. This brotherhood must be made concrete in the community.[67]

Now it is necessary to look at Shepherding as it encourages the existential human condition in churches today.

NOTES

[1]Dulles, *Models of the Church*, p. 152.

[2]W.E. Vine, *An Expository Dictionary of New Testament Words*, 4 vols. (Old Tappan, New Jersey: Fleming Revell Co., 1966), 3:212.

[3]Gerhard Kittel, ed., *Theological Dictionary of the New Testament*, 10 vols. (Grand Rapids: Eerdmans Pub. Co., 1964-76), vol. 3: *Hierateuma* by Gottlob (1966), p. 251.

[4]Oscar Feucht, *Everyone A Minister* (St. Louis: Concordia Publishing House, 1974), p. 40.

[5]J. Robert Wright, "Canterbury Statement and the Five Priesthoods, *Anglican Theological Review* S 7 (October 1975): 450.

[6]Donald Nash, "Clergy," *Voice of Kentucky Christian College* 3 (October 1977): 20-4.

[7]Feucht, *Everyone a Minister,* p. 74.

[8]*Ibid.*

[9]I recognize that this view is not universally accepted among Christian circles. It is, however, the conclusion I draw from exegeting Biblical passages.

[10]All Biblical quotations are from the Revised Standard version unless stated otherwise.

[11]Cyril Eastwood, *Royal Priesthood of the Faithful* (Minneapolis: Augsburg Publishing House, 1963), p. 2.

[12]E. Best, *Spiritual Sacrifices in General Priesthood in the New Testament* "Novum Testamentum 11 (1969): 41:276.

[13]Eastwood, *The Royal Priesthood of the Faithful*, p. 3.

[14]*Ibid.*, pp. 18, 19.

[15]Elton Trueblood, *The Incendiary Fellowship* (New York: Harper & Row, 1967), p. 39.

[16]Mark Gibbs & T. Ralph Morton, *God's Frozen People* (Philadelphia: Westminster Press, 1964), p. 14.

[17]Paul Benjamin, *The Growing Congregation* (Lincoln, Illinois: Lincoln Christian College Press, 1972), p. 25.

[18]E. Best, "I Peter 2:4-10 A Reconsideration," *Novum Testamentum* 11 (1969)? 4:273.

[19]Feucht, *Everyone A Minister*, p. 37.

[20]Best, "I Peter 2:4-10," p. 284.

[21]*Ibid.*, p. 288.

[22]Feucht, *Everyone a Minister*, p. 39.

[23]John Elliot, "Death of a Slogan; from Royal Priest to Celebrating community," *Una Sancta* 3 (1968): 25:19.

[24]Eastwood, *The Priesthood of all Believers*, p. 79.

[25]Feucht, *Everyone a Minister*, pp. 36, 37.

[26]Elliot, "Death of a Slogan," p. 25.

[27]Larry Richards, *Regions Beyond* (Fullerton, California: David C. Cook, 1977), p. 109.

[28]Hiltner, *Ferment in Ministry*, p. 34.

[29]S.L. Greenslade, *Shepherding the Flock* (Naperville, Illinois: SCM Book Club, 1967), pp. 31, 42.

[30]Benjamin, *The Growing Congregation*, p. 31.

[31]Eastwood, *The Priesthood of Believers*, p. 12.

[32]Other Scriptures related to the Priesthood of Believers are briefly annotated at the end of this work.

[33]Eastwood, *The Royal Priesthood of the Faithful*, p. 56-80.

[34]Lars Qualben, *A History of the Christian Church* (New York: Thomas Nelson & Sons, 1950) p. 127.

[35]Norman Ullestad, "The Priesthood of Believers Plans for Tomorrow" (D. Min. Disquisition, Wartburg Theological Society, 1976), p. 2.

[36]For Luther's view of the church and ministry refer to the notes at the end of the chapter.

[37]Eastwood, *Priesthood of Believers*, p. 3.

[38]*Ibid.*, p. 43.

[39]Ullestad, "The Priesthood of Believers Plans for Tomorrow," p. 3.

[40]Eastwood, *Priesthood of Believers*, p. 90.

[41]*Ibid.*, p. 70.

[42]For an excellent exegetical and word study analysis of the Priesthood of Believers see E. Best, "Spiritual Sacrifices in General Priesthood in the New Testament," *Interpretation* 273 (July 1960): 14:99.

[43]Hiltner, *The Christian Shepherd*, pp. 14, 15.

[44]Vine, *An Expository Dictionary of New Testament Words*, 4:19.

[45]*Ibid.*, 3:167.

[46]According to Moulton and Geden (p. 831) this is every instance of the noun. The verb is found in Matthew 2:6; Luke 17:7; John 21:16; Acts 20:28; I Corinthians 9:7; I Peter 5:2; Revelation 2:27; 7:17; 12:5; 19:15. The term "flock" is found in Luke 12:23; Acts 20:28, 29; I Peter 5:2, 3.

[47]This could be translated, "The Lord is my Pastor." In Psalm 80:1, God is seen as the Shepherd of Israel.

[48]Adams, *Pastoral Leadership*, pp. 6, 7.

[49]Francis MacNutt, *Healing* (Notre Dame, Indiana: Ave Maria Press, 1974), p. 161f.

[50]See also I Peter 2:25; Hebrews 13:17; Acts 20:28, 30.

[51]See also John 10:14, 15; Revelation 7:17; John 21:15-19.

[52]"The Shepherd image is used quite often in the Old Testament to describe the relationship between Yahweh and His covenant people as a group (Isaiah 40:11; Ezekiel 34:10; Psalm 80:1)." A. Rohr Von Saver, "Fact and Image in the Shepherd Psalm," *Concordia Theological Monthly* 42 (September 1971): 488-92.

[53]Martin Francis, "Image of Shepherd in the Gospel of St. Matthew," *Science Et Esprit* 27 (October-December 1975): 261-301.

[54]*Ibid.*, pp. 275, 276.

[55]*Ibid.*, p. 284.

[56]Matthew 12:22-30 and 15:21-28 are similar in their effect. Matthew 14:14 and 20:29-34 use the same term *"splagchnizomai"* (compassion) as in 9:36 thus heightening the healing motif. *"Splagchna"* literally, "the bowls", were regarded by the Greeks as the seat of the more violent passions and by the Hebrews as the seat of the tender affections. Vine, *Dictionary of New Testament Words* 1:37, 37. On page 901 Moulton and Geden we find the New Testament uses of the term "compassion".

verb: *splagchnizomai*

noun: *splagchnon*

Matthew 9:39	Mark 6:34	Luke 1:78	Philemon 7
Matthew 14:14	Mark 8:2	Acts 1:18	Philemon 12
Matthew 15:32	Mark 9:22	II Cor. 6:12	Philemon 20
Matthew 18:27	Luke 7:13	II Cor. 7:15	I John 3:17
Mark 20:34	Luke 10:33	Philippians 2:1	
Mark 1:41	Luke 15:20	Colossians 3:12	

These tender affections lead people from sensitivity to action. Shepherds in God's church would do well to possess this compassion.

[57]*Ibid.*, p. 284.

[58]This healing is also found in the Old Testament. Zechariah 11:15-17 and Jeremiah 23:2 delcare that God cares for the flock by healing the wounded, tending them, gathering together and the like. *Paqad* "visit" and *Episkepto* (LXX) show that while the idea of vistation (as it is usually conceived) is not necessarily bound up with

Shepherds, there is a vital sense in which the two are peculiarly connected. The "visitation" in view in both the Old and New Testaments at its core is oversight that shows concern for. Adams, *The Pastoral Life*, p. 75.

[59]Francis Schaeffer, *The Church at the End of the 20th Century* (Downers Grove, Illinois: Inter-Varsity Press, 1970), pp. 152, 153.

[60]Hiltner, *The Christian Shepherd*, p. 16.

[61]*Ibid.*, p. 18.

[62]Shedd, *Pastoral Ministry*, p. 13.

[63]See W.F. Lown, "On Feeding Sheep," *Christian Shepherd* (April 18, 1976), p. 13.

[64]See Edith Schaeffer, "Hospitality: Optional or Commanded," *Christian Standard* (December 17, 1976), pp. 28, 29.

[65]Shedd, *Pastoral Ministry*, p. 14.

[66]See Andrew Hairston, "The Kingdom Meets Human Needs," *Christian Standard* (March 28, 1976), pp. 5-7.

[67]Hans Küng, *Why Priests? A Proposal for a New Church Ministry* (Garden City, N.Y.: Doubleday, 1972), pp. 33, 34.

CHAPTER II

DIAGNOSIS OF THE NECESSITY AND PROBLEMS OF SHEPHERDING

*"One can acquire everything in solitude
except character."*

Stendahl

NEEDS

Fundamental to my hermeneutical base is the assumption that the Bible was written to record God's dealings with the needs of man. Therefore, the theme of Shepherding as described in the previous chapter arose because the needs of man dictated the necessity of Shepherding. My bias is that man is basically the same today as in the first century and has similar needs. As needs resulted in biblical instruction to deal with that lacking, so the biblical material will adequately satisfy the cravings of twentieth century man. In other words, because man's basic needs are the same, the biblical concept of Shepherding is just as valid today as it was in the first century. What is necessary, therefore, in my opinion, is to articulate some of these human experiences which need healing, i.e. Shepherding.

The distresses of people are varied and entail multiplicities of relationships. Many people need the church's ministry: the physically ill, emotionally ill, bereaved, aged and lonely, marital problems, parent-child problems, alcoholism,[1] and unemployment.

These existential human conditions need healing and often the sufferer needs guiding. The Shepherding Model is designed by God in the Scriptures and through this program to help people deal with and work through these problems. The Gospel command to heal gives us the basis for the Shepherding task.[2]

Even more basic to the premise of the above situations, however, is man's need to be loved and accepted unconditionally. Each person has a fundamental need to act effectively in the world and to be judged by rigorous standards of appraisal and evaluation.[3] The uniqueness of a Shepherding Program in the church is that it comes from the Body of Christ which acknowledges and expects compliance with the standards of God, yet demonstrates accepting those (all of us) who fall below this standard. These fundamental needs of love, acceptance, and performance are, therefore, met.

ISSUES

Without attempting a sociological study of cultural trends it is helpful to look at some phenomena in our society which help contribute to Shepherding as one way to meet people's needs. As individualism has increased so has the lack of community concern increased. In a neighborhood of young families hardly anyone expects to live there permanently. There exists today little sense of the larger community.[4] This fact tends to isolate people and fragment relationships. The fundamental needs previously expressed often go unmet. Furthermore, specialization compounds isolation and fragmentation. Often the individualization has enriched competency in one area at the loss of relationship.

The Shepherding Model of sustaining addresses itself to this problem. Relationships are sustained while unity and continuity of relationships are offered. The point is that though neighborhoods, work situations, and society may change and cause isolation, the Shepherding function in the Body of Christ draws people together in the Lord.

Individual churches have reasons of their own to develop a Shepherding Program. The size of the congregation is a very significant factor. As the church becomes larger there is more of a chance for people to get "lost in the crowd." Isolation becomes more of an unfortunate possibility the more people there are to relate to. My personal experience verified this as I came to a larger church when moving into a new community during my college days. I was "alone in the crowd." Such a feeling evokes loneliness and fear. The problem, of course, is the impossibility of one person or even a few people to meaningfully relate to a large number of people. The Shepherding Model is based upon the precept of "My Shepherd." In Psalm 23 the personal pronoun (I-(I-My) is used some seventeen times. No minister or group of elders can give the personal touch in the degree needed for spiritual growth to every member of the congregation. An intimate personal relationship is needed. Though the program is limited even in this area by shepherd functioning and peoples' responses, the design is addressed to this issue.

Another factor, which Beloit Central Christian experiences, is that members of the congregation arise from as many as six communities or cities. The people come together for worship but go their separate ways until the next Lord's Day — or even longer. Under such circumstances it is difficult to develop a family atmosphere or a body-like functioning. The

Shepherd Model attempts to draw the Body of Christ together. These contacts help bring unity beyond the Sunday morning worship service and to solidify the community of faith.

One more contributing factor to a church's fragmentation is the experience of a "church split." Such an incident often causes feelings of hurt, alienation, distrust, and anxiety. These feelings are not only evident between members of the different factions but also within the "aligned" groups. Shepherding in all its aspects — healing, sustaining, and guiding — directs its efforts to assist in working through the feelings enumerated. Real care can help bandage past wounds. As this ministry continues, it can in time relieve much of the pain. One must certainly recognize the slow process involved here, but if healing is not fostered then the relationships can only fester as a laceration left uncleaned.

The specific reasons for Shepherding are as numerous as the needs of a congregation. Man living in a fallen sinful world has a multitude of sins to cover. Every congregation would have to design a Shepherding Program to meet its particular situation. However, my conviction is that this program addresses itself to the basic problem areas of pastoral ministry.

When sharing the Beloit program with a Bible College Professor, I was almost apologetic about its need. My deep-down conviction was that such a program should not be necessary, for such ministry should be a spontaneous outgrowth of Christian life. The professor expressed to me, however, that living a Christian life and performing pastoral ministry is not natural. They need to be learned. The program has some justification because of its educational nature. It teaches people how to heal, to sustain, and to guide.

Even more fundamental, however, programmed shepherding ideally presents a model of Christian life for the rest of the community of faith to emulate. The ultimate goal of this program is to motivate and to activate every member of the congregation to shepherd his fellow believers. The structure is not intended to classify Christians but to utilize modeling as a means to educate and to stimulate the people of God.

Theologically speaking one might state that didactic means and grace are involved. In II Timothy 2:2 Paul writes, "And the things you have heard me say in the presence of many witnesses entrust to reliable men who will also be qualified to teach others." This program attempts to do this with the hope that the teaching will "snowball." Furthermore, Paul, after expressing that salvation is through grace and a gift of God, communicates in Ephesians 2:10 that the result of grace is that Christians were "created in Christ Jesus to do good works, which God prepared us in advance for us to do." The Shepherding Model gives expression to these good works.

Another reason for shepherd development is that people (church) often know what should be done but have no idea how to do it. My experience has led me to believe that the majority of the people who belong to the community of faith want to contribute a meaningful service. Their fear is aroused, however, about their ability to do something. Two important factors are involved in this issue. First, those who are mature in the faith are to assist those in need. In Titus 2:4ff Paul encourages the older women to "train the young women to love their husbands and children, to be sensible, chaste, domestic, kind, and submissive to their husbands." Who can be of better assistance to a person needing direction that a mother or father in the faith? Shepherds, therefore, need a degree of maturity, concern, and desire to help train.

The second factor to be considered is the matter of spiritual gifts. God, through the Holy Spirit, has given gift(s) to his people individually (I Corinthians 12:4-11). Very often a brother[5] is not able to discern for himself what gift he has. The observation of a fellow Christian may well be a revelation and an affirmation of confidence to a searching soul. The benefit of "I believe you can do . . ." or "It seems God has given you the gift to . . ." cannot be measured. Once a person is aware that he can, he is usually more favorable to explore how. A sensitive shepherd can aid in giving some greatly needed direction.

God has designed the physical body to function on its own. The various parts complement one another and assist each other in performing their duties. The eyes, nose, tongue, mouth, arm, hand, and brain work together to bring nourishment into their body. In like manner, God has constructed the Body of Christ, the church. The different parts of this Body also have a responsibility to each other for mutual fulfillment (I Corinthians 12:7). The abilities, gifts, and potential are innate to the community. The grace of God has seen to that. All that is needed is a catalyst to motivate and activate what God has given. The Shepherding program of pastoral care by the body's members is designed to execute this mutual gratification.

Without being overly simplistic, "ownership" is the redeeming element of Shepherding. Most people take more pride and interest in something they own than in something they use. A house or care which has been secured through one's hard and persistent labor is very dear to one's heart. Owning such an item tends to cause a person to be a little more particular and careful with it. Watching the actions and reactions of a teenager who purchases his own automobile often demonstrates this truth. Many examples can be thought of which generally support the validity of this view.

My contention is that as the above is true in purely physical things so it is true in ministry. Within the church, the community will support those programs and ministries which they own. As Christ's body works together to determine service, they will perform that service. In contrast, however, as regulations, expectations, and requirements are "laid on" people, they often resent what "the pastor" or "the board" has outlined for them to do.

Ownership in this sense, therefore is the decision making of taking responsibility. When the church plans and decides for itself, she is more likely to be involved. My experience has been that "the Minister's Program" is often not as exciting and meaningful as "our program." The minister or small group may be the catalyst, and the Lord knows how we need that within most churches, but programs which really succeed ultimately become a "grass roots" movement. When the church, as a whole, believes in something and works for it, the program will succeed. Often, however, time is necessary for the grass roots to be stirred.

Ephesians 4:11-13 states:

> . . . it was he who gave some to be apostles, some to be prophets, some to be evangelists, and some to be pastors and teachers, to prepare God's people for works of service, so that the Body of Christ may be built up until we all reach unity in the faith and in the knowledge of the Son of God and become mature, attaining the full measure of perfection found in Christ. (NIV)

The leadership is to activate all God's people for the work of the ministry. Unless the whole church is involved in the total ministry, the work will not get done. Each person is to become mature. However, in the majority of churches one person (pastor) does not have the time or physical and spiritual abilities (much to the deflating of some egos) to develop that level of maturity in every member. Therefore, the whole body needs to help one another. This ministry not only fulfills this Scripture, but it also develops ownership for the church's ministry.

The Shepherding Program is a step in that direction. By no means is it a panacea for all the body's ills. By no means has this program successfully developed complete ownership within the church. However, it is a step forward for it involves more people in decision-making and ownership, and it serves as a model of Christian behavior and ministry. Children frequently mimic and become what they observe; children of faith often do the same. Hopefully, the ministry of Shepherding will develop churchwide healing, sustaining, and guiding.

Programs are to serve people, not people serve programs. When ownership is developed, then programs will serve the needs of people. Such problems as lazy shepherds, opposition to being shepherded, etc. can be dealt with by the group and the elders for they own the ministry. More will be shared about this issue in the discussion about organization.

A point that I constantly must be reminded of is that the Christian life is one of becoming. One never attains perfection. Spiritual growth is a journey filled with valleys and mountains. Time is required for growing. The development, implementation, and excellence of such a program is a constantly shifting matter. Time is also needed for the cultivation and production of desired results. The Beloit program is becoming : "Please be patient, God isn't done with me yet."

NOTES

[1]Samuel Southard, *Comprehensive Pastoral Care* (Valley Forge: Jedson Press, 1975), p. 41.

[2]Hiltner, *Christian Shepherd*, p. 103.

[3]John Biersdorf, ed. *Creating an Intentional Ministry* (Nashville: Abingdon, 1976) p. 32.

[4]Hiltner, *Christian Shepherd*, p. 103.

[5]All these statements include women too. The masculine gender will be used for simplicity's sake, but in no way is exclusive. All Christians, regardless of sex, are called to be priests and to perform the ministry of healing through Shepherding.

CHAPTER III

Planning a Shepherding Program

*"The beginning is half of the whole,
and we all praise a good beginning."*
Plato

A MODEL

Where does one begin in planning a Shepherding Program? Hopefully, the two previous chapters have demonstrated the biblical precedent and injunction for pastoral care. With this background, therefore, a logical place for me to begin is in creating a model, having a biblical foundation, which directs itself to the needs of one's particular congregation. Jay Adams[1] portrays two contrasting organizational patterns which exist today. I prefer the one he has described as the "Biblical Pattern" and have attempted to utilize it in planning our Shepherding care. This model is illustrated on the following page.

This pattern puts into practice the Priesthood of Believer's Doctrine. Evangelicals generally agree with this theory. Almost every college course on church history credits Martin Luther with its revival. The existence of this priesthood is generally recognized in Christendom but few provisions are structured into the church for it.[2]

After considering such options as multiple staff, the Eldership of Beloit Central and I agreed upon the following organizational pattern to present to the congregation.

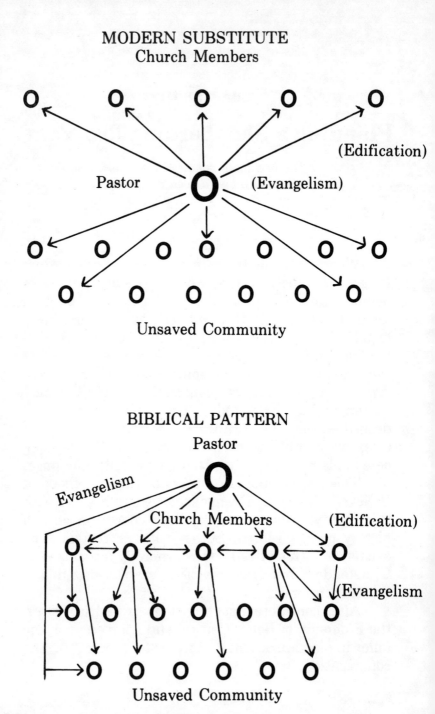

MODERN SUBSTITUTE
Church Members

(Edification)

Pastor
(Evangelism)

Unsaved Community

BIBLICAL PATTERN
Pastor

Evangelism

Church Members
(Edification)

(Evangelism

Unsaved Community

SITUATION

Our congregation consists of some two hundred sixty (260) families. These families include just one person (e.g., single, widowed, divorced), one person from a family, or a several member family. People who regularly attend the church for a period of three months, even though they are not members, are also included. These people are added only after they give consent to be included. All members are automatically listed. If only one person in the family is a member or regularly attending, the whole family unit is shepherded as the need arises. However, anyone who refuses assistance is not coerced. Members and non-members have the right to decline shepherding. A more opportune time may occur later. Therefore, no one is just written off.

With two hundred sixty families including some six hundred people, it is impossible for any one person to shepherd them all. Each member is called to be a pastor to somebody. Every Christian contacts someone with questions which demand answers. The trouble with the ordinary pastoral system is that it does not go far enough. There can be no vital church without a multipastoral system![3] A Shepherding Program provides that multiple system.

The formula that the Elders and I arrived at was that a Shepherd should not have more than eight (8) families to which to minister. The general rule is for every Shepherd to care for six (6) to eight (8) family units. This number of units generally consists of twenty (20) or more individuals. In our opinion that is plenty. It is my judgment that an ideal number of families would be four (4). The time element involved would not be so great. However, that has not become a reality in our situation.

Of the thirty-six shepherds, six are Elders of the congregation. These men are elected by the congregation to oversee and guide the church (Acts 20:17-38; I Peter 5:1-5). The Elder's responsibility is two-fold in this program:

(1) To oversee the ministry of the Shepherds. This means that they supervise the Shepherds' efforts and assist them in any way possible. The elders may call with the Shepherds or be resource people for advice and guidance. The elders certainly have the opportunity and responsibility to sustain and guide the Shepherds. In essence, the elders are in charge of the program.

(2) To be Shepherds of the Shepherds. The elders, therefore, perform the same ministry[4] for the Shepherds that the Shepherds perform for those on their lists. Each elder, therefore, has approximately four Shepherd families on his list.[5]

The Shepherds are selected on the basis of desire and competency for ministry. Men, women, or couples may be Shepherds. My opinion is that couples are ideal. Couples can then relate to other couples and usually have greater flexibility of time due to work schedules. However, this is not always possible. Widowed women and even the divorced are frequently excellent Shepherds because of their past experiences. Certainly, any helping person is a wounded healer, but some are able to heal more effectively because they have experienced a similar wound. Contingent upon the approval of the elders, any Christian individual is a Shepherd candidate.

ORGANIZATION AND LISTINGS

The initial organization of the lists were by geographical location. If possible, a Shepherd was selected in close proximity. This was especially true of groups outside Beloit. Some shepherding plans call these zones. Our experience demonstrated that definite geographical lines could not be kept. The factors were too varied: Shepherds change, people move, death eliminates, personality conflicts, and new members do not always "choose" the right area in which to live. Neighborhood Shepherding groups are advantageous, but in such a mobile society the necessity is not as great as in years past. Flexibility is definitely the rule of this organization.

To enhance reference availability the Shepherding lists were arranged in two manners: according to Shepherd and according to family. The listings according to Shepherds allow for the immediate referral to whomever is on each Shepherd's list and which elder is the overseer. The list according to family quickens ascertainment of the Shepherd in case of a need. These lists are available to anyone who wants them but are distributed to every elder and Shepherd. As a rule, the communication network for relaying needs and lists is through the church office because the information usually goes there first. Hopefully, in time, more direct relationship will take place between a Shepherd and "his people." Following are fictitious lists as described above. Every member is on a Shepherding list. This includes the Shepherd, elders, and pastors.

Shepherding List
According to Shepherd

1. Sally Anderson
John Brown
Lois Crane
Tom Friar
Charles Meaney
Geraldine Stone
Howard Voice
Sue Williams
James Zephyr

2. George Bane
Sam Austin
Dan Boone
Mary Miller
Ronald Niemoller
D.J. Pointers
Peter Simon
Andrew Yellow

3. Sue Dickson

James Alphanus	Mary Magdala
Ken Engles	John Moonies
Wayne Fingers	Leah Sanderson
Alice Fry	John Zebedee

Shepherding List
According to Family

	Shepherd
ALPHANUS, JAMES	Sue Dickson
AUSTIN, SAM	George Bane
BOONE, DAN	George Bane
BROWN, John	Sally Anderson
CRANE, Lois	Sally Anderson
ENGLES, Ken	Sue Dickson
FINGERS, Wayne	Sue Dickson
FRIAR, Tom	Sally Anderson
FRY, Alice	Sue Dickson
MAGDALA, Mary	Sue Dickson
MEANEY, Charles	Sally Anderson
MOONIES, John	Sue Dickson
NIEMOLLER Ron	George Bane
POINTERS, D.J.	George Bane
SANDERSON, Leah	Sue Dickson
SIMON, Peter	George Bane

GOALS

Proverbs 29:18 states, "Where there is no vision the people perish." The truth of this statement is confirmed by nations, businesses, schools, and churches. The Shepherding Program must have a goal. James Gunn in his chapter, "Goal-Setting and Evaluation," defines goal-setting as translating a vision into a specific description of a desired state of affairs.[6] Goal-setting brings vision into practical living. The specific goals of the Beloit Central Christian project are expressed in the job description found in the next chapter. The general goal is for "lay" people to be actively reaching into the homes of the people of the community week by week. Preaching, formal teaching, or an occasional evangelistic drive cannot take the place of this kind of pastoral ministry.[7] Hopefully, the Model of Shepherding (healing, sustaining, guiding) will become a lifestyle for the whole Priesthood of Believers.

Goals, in my experience, are not static. The job description now may not be the job description one or five years from now. As the congregation journeys through life, so will her specific needs. Different congregations will begin and progress at various levels and with diversified needs. Goals are, therefore, a process. Each congregation must establish its own specific goals. Meaningful goals are very often articulated through the experience of evaluation rather than designed on first chance.[8] For this reason the chapter on "Evaluations" is very significant, for these times of the program's soul-searching directly relate to the goals.

My belief is that the Beloit program can provide a sounding board, measuring stick, and example for other congregations to formulate from and modify for their particular constituency. The goals we have set have not been completely fulfilled. Other possible goals will be enumerated as hopeful future developments. We are in the process of becoming.

STEPS FOR PRESENTATION

In presenting the concept of Shepherding to the Beloit congregation, I discussed the matter initially with the elders. In my opinion the elders have the responsibility of the spiritual oversight and pastoral care of the congregation. Their support is, therefore, mandatory under our system of communication and authority. With their approval I presented the program to the whole Board (consisting of elders and deacons and now trustees). Upon their acceptance, the concepts were shared with the congregation through our newsletter, from the pulpit, and by one to one discussion with many members. The vote for adoption was through a consensus of the board, not a congregational meeting. Those of the congregation who were personally confronted with the program responded favorably expressing that the concept should have been implemented long ago.[9] The time involved from inception to implementation was about four months.

As I presented the programs to the above people, I realized a format would be helpful. Furthermore, I was invited to share the program at a Christian Education Clinic,[10] a sister congregation in Footville, a United Methodist Church,[11] and was invited to assist in conducting a workshop at the North American Christian Convention.[12] These presentations necessitated the formulation of the format which is listed as Appendix I. The steps outlined are in essence the same as the chapters of this book. I have found it comprehensive enough for all the situations discussed. Any items not covered for individuals arise in the discussions which are a part of each sharing. These discussions often resulted in minor modifications.

The modifications given by elders, deacons, church members, and Shepherds are significant because these changes are putting the Priesthood of Believers Doctrine into practice. The whole church has the right and responsibility for the formation and process of the program. This fact will become more evident as the evaluative procedures are discussed.

SUMMARY

The planning of a Shepherding program takes organization in set-up, in preparing goals, and in presentation. The planning of these steps is an essential foundation to the success of the program. Furthermore, it is crucial to the fulfillment of the Priesthood of Believers Doctrine and to the concept of ministry ownership by the church.

Each of the concepts discussed intertwines; one without the other loses its balance or creates a false facade. These old words hold true in this context: "Form without content is pretense. Content without form is piffle."[13]

NOTES

[1]Adams, *Pastoral Leadership*, p. 28.

[2]Robert Girard, *Brethren, Hang Loose* (Grand Rapids, 1972), p. 86. These seven principles of New Testament church life have guided our Heritage Church as she has sought to rediscover in century twenty the vibrant life of the Christian fellowship of century one:

(1) Depend on Holy Spirit instead of "the flesh".
(2) Concentrate on the maturing of Christians.
(3) Recognize the priesthood of all believers.
(4) Build the church fellowship around Christ.
(5) Release church life from the confines of the church building.

(6) Recognize our place in the total Body of Christ.

(7) Build church unity on the basis of love.

[3]Trueblood, *The Incendary Fellowship*, p. 54.

[4]A job description will be discussed in the next chapter.

[5]It should be noted that every elder is on a Shepherd's list. This is also true of the paid ministers.

[6]John Biersdorf, ed. *Creating an Intentional Ministry* (Nashville: Abingdon, 1976), p. 127.

[7]Feucht, *Everyone a Minister*, p. 110.

[8]Biersdorf, *Creating an Intentional Ministry*, p. 127.

[9]As time progressed and as the program was implemented it was ascertained that some, but not very many, did not understand the program's purpose or helpfulness.

[10]This Clinic was held in Janesville with about six congregations present.

[11]In Roscoe, Illinois, where Dr. Richard Boyer was pastor.

[12]This convention is a national preaching and teaching gathering of the independent Christian Churches. No policies or church business are legislated at such conventions. This was held in Cincinnati, Ohio. About 25,000 people attended the total convention and some 200 at the workshop I helped conduct.

[13]This statement was first conveyed to me by Professor Charles Mills at Lincoln Christian College.

CHAPTER IV

Shepherding Development

"Everyman's work is a portrait of himself."
Samuel Butler

In presenting the Shepherding model of ministry a very important aspect is the sharing of the responsibilities of the Shepherds. For the first nine months of the program no written job description was available. The duties were merely explained by myself or the elders. I came to the realization, however, that the Shepherds did not have any ownership of their duties. In fact, the elders and I laid down the responsibilities and expected the Shepherds to fulfill them. This practice was just the opposite of the ministry's central concept: the priesthood and shared responsibility of all believers. Therefore, at the initiative of one of the Shepherds, a whole evening was devoted to the formulation of a "job description."

To give a starting point, I listed the responsibilities which had been verbally accepted by the Shepherds. I then strongly stressed that they had the option to trim, modify, or add any responsibilities they deemed necessary. The following job description is the fruit of that effort as we broke into groups of four and five and then reconvened for a composite picture.

SHEPHERD JOB DESCRIPTION
Central Christian Church
Beloit, Wisconsin

(1) Maintain personal touch every six to eight weeks.

(2) Visit in case of sickness or death.

(3) Help find areas of service.

(4) Act as telephone committee.

(5) Assist in distributing sheets.

(6) Offer one's services.

These responsibilities are further explained in the following paragraphs. I have also added editorial comments, not in the printed "job description" given to each Shepherd as seen in Appendix II.

(1) Personal Contact

Contact is defined as "talking to the person." This can be done in a face to face encounter or on the telephone. Contacts could be made at worship services, casually on the street or at stores, during special church or community activities, or through special calls because of sickness, death, or extended absenteeism. The important factor is to let people know they are remembered and cared for. One of the above contacts is to be made every six to eight weeks.

If a person does not respond positively, the Shepherd is to try again. If there is still no satisfactory response, he is to wait for a special contact such as an anniversary celebration, sickness, or death in the family. The attempt is to create personalism. Jesus said, "I know my sheep and they know me." Personal contact will also assist in formulating the church into the body and family of Christ. Guiding and sustaining can more readily be actualized when a personal relationship has been cultivated.[1]

(2) Sickness or Death

Upon learning of sickness (usually the church office will call), the Shepherd should send a card immediately. The minister or church office will advise whether a visit is appropriate or not. This practice is considered because some people do not desire visitors while others may not be able to welcome visitors (intensive care, isolation). If the person cannot be seen, it is suggested that a family member be contacted to relay concern and to see how the church can minister to the family. If at all possible, the Shepherd should visit or phone (if advisable) a hospital patient.

In case of death in the family, the Shepherd will make a personal visit at the person's home, at night visitation at the funeral home, or by coming to the funeral service. A sympathy card should also be sent.

The ministry of healing is enacted in this guideline. Sickness and death involve healing of the body, soul, emotions, and relationships. At these delicate moments people are often more open to pastoral care than at any other time. Furthermore, when someone besides "the pastor" performs the healing ministry, it is often very meaningful because it is not "expected." These times are definitely opportunities to "weep with those who weep" and to share their common faith.

(3) Areas of Service

Frequently, members of the church relay to each other areas where they would like to serve the church but do not tell the minister or elders. The Shepherd can assist greatly in this area by passing the word along. Furthermore, as the Shepherd grows in his relationship with his people, he may see that the person has abilities or interests which could be used in the church. This information can also be passed along, for the elders may not know of these abilities or interests and have not considered the person for some particular service.

The actualization of the Universal Priesthood is a goal of this responsibility. The discovering of gifts and interests is a vital step in realizing this goal. Every person has something to contribute to God's church (I Corinthians 12). Performing this contribution brings satisfaction and fulfillment. Guiding is an important phase of Shepherding in this area. The hope is to bring every person into "mature manhood."[2]

(4) Telephone Committee

The Shepherding program is a built-in network of communication for the congregation. Telephoning the complete congregation may be necessary in cases of special prayers, congregational business meetings, revival services, or appointments for such things as a church directory. By having the Shepherds call, it is possible to contact the whole congregation in a short period of time without placing too heavy a burden on anyone.

Body and family life result from communications with the various parts. This network provides a "nerve system" for the congregation. Quick, vital messages are easily relayed. When utilized, it makes each person feel like being a part of the whole.

The procedure would be for the church office to contact the elders, the elders to call the Shepherds under their oversight, and for the Shepherds to call their people. In this manner no one person makes more than eight calls.

(5) Questionnaire Distribution

At times the church surveys congregational talent and interest, evaluations of various programs of the congregation, or other written responses. It has been found that the congregation participates more fully when personally confronted with these sheets than when the information is simply placed in the church paper or bulletin. The Shepherd's responsibility would be to get the sheet to his people and pick it up (or make other arrangements) from them. This process also allows opportunity to make a contact.

Sheet (questionnaire) distribution has the same basis as the last two areas. The whole church is contacted for evaluation and services in an attempt to create a priesthood and a body life.

Of course, some people choose not to participate, and that decision is respected. However, our experience has borne out that personal contact by the Shepherds creates more participation than if the sheets are distributed in the mail or worship service. In 1974 the congregation was sent "talent and survey sheets" in the "Evangel" (weekly newsletter). Twelve were returned. In 1976 the Shepherds distributed and gathered one hundred fifty. Though this figure does not involve the total membership, it is a significant increase! We are "becoming!"

(6) Offering Services

Shepherds are to communicate their availability to help the person when in need. Some Shepherds have given the people rides to the doctor, helped fix cars, baked pies, etc. It is suggested that each family have the Shepherd's name, address, and telephone number.

The Shepherding model of healing, sustaining, and guiding is a live option in this responsibility. The ministry is to the total man. The New Testament Church attempted to meet any need which arose because of brotherly love and concern. We are attempting to do the same.

An extremely important statement is made by Jay Adams which needs consideration about a job description. "It is not a job description only, but also a job accomplishment that you want to convey by your remarks. Your stress should not be upon function, but upon purpose; not so much how (that must come later) but upon what."[3]

When the function and accomplishment are stressed and accepted, reliable Shepherds will result. Real Shepherds are called, not hired. Jesus pointed to this fact after identifying Himself as the Good Shepherd (John 10:11-15). When it comes to the "nitty-gritty ' of service, hirelings are more interested in saving their own skins than ministering to the sheep.[4] Clarification of the expectations can assure more "real Shepherds."[5]

Our Shepherds felt that more than just functions needed enumeration. The following concerns helped clarify the exact status of the Shepherd.

(7) People Responsible For

Each Shepherd is responsible to care for six to eight families. These families either have at least one person who is a member of the church or the family has been attending regularly for about three months. The list each Shepherd has may change due to additions of new members, deletions from moving away or death, or exchanging with a different Shepherd for personal reasons. These changes will only be done when necessary and with the consent of the elders and minister.

(8) Chain of Responsibility

Ultimately every Christian is responsible to God. The Shepherding Program is not tightly or strictly controlled, but each Shepherd will be assigned to an elder who will oversee his work. The minister will also closely work with each Shepherd.

(9) Term

The time of service is one year beginning September 1 of each year. At this time a Shepherd may continue, terminate, or exchange lists with another Shepherd. This latter alternative will be done with the consent of the elders and minister.

(10) Training

Through the course of each year there will be approximately three seminars with Shepherds in mind. If at all possible, it is hoped that each Shepherd will attend these training sessions to increase his capacity for ministry. The elders and minister are also always available for consultation.

(11) Enlistment

The securing of Shepherds is a very significant procedure. Part of the Shepherding concept is to cause the church to understand that it is not an agency to be served, but a work force to be deployed. Unfortunately, the work force is often small and static.[6] It seems that the same core does all the work. However, our experience broadened that generalization and several "additional" members became involved. Our hope is to expand further for few individuals can participate effectively on more than two levels of institutional structure.[7]

The procedure followed in Beloit can be categorized in two broad areas with specific methods under each.

    (A) Explain the program and ask for volunteers

        (1) The newsletter ("Evangel") and the Sunday bulletin were used for this. A brief explanation of the nature of the program was shared with directives to talk to the elders or myself.

        (2) From the pulpit the main points of Shepherding were enumerated and a call

for Shepherds was extended. A sermon or a series of sermons about the Ministry of Shepherding could have helped clarify to the congregation the theological foundations for this ministry and its need. I did not do this at the program's beginning but have done so since then.

From this method six Shepherds were secured in two weeks.

(B) Talk to specific individuals

    (1) The people consulted resulted from suggestions by the elders. As the overseers of the church and this ministry, they are responsible for the quality of Shepherds. The elders, therefore, with myself, studied the church membership for qualified and hopefully willing people. Each of us spoke to some. As a rule, however, I did most of the contacting.

    (2) These people were also considered due to previous talent survey sheets. This was not very helpful, for few sheets were on file when the program began. However, since more sheets are on file because of the program its usage is somewhat more valuable.

From this personal contact the remainder of the Shepherds were pledged. Our experience demonstrated that individual explanation and commitment is much more effective and lasting.[8] Within another month and a half the list was complete. The planning and enlistment as discussed to this point took about four months.

(12) Seminars

The fear of many people is their lack of skills for

ministry. This fear may be well-founded, but stress
has been laid upon the desire to minister and to listen
to people.

Security in ministry grows as competency is
increased. Training sessions were and are, therefore,
planned to increase competency in ministry. The
following examples were training sessions along with
their leaders and dates.

1976
August 14 Dr. Hilliard Comeaux Communication Skills
(Minnesota Bible College)

1977
January 13, Dr. Richard Boyer Leadership Development
20, 27,   (Roscoe, Illinois United Methodist Church)
February 3

April 15-17   Roger Smelser   Spirit-filled Life
(Wisconsin State Evangelist)

August 20 Dr. Hilliard Comeaux Communications Skills
(Minnesota Bible College) (calling in homes)

1978
September 17-19   Roger Smelser Personal Evangelism
(Wisconsin State Evangelist)

The goals of these seminars were to increase skills
in listening, counseling, leading, and scriptural
understanding. In my estimation they were successful
in reaching the desired goals.

In addition to inviting outside personnel, I
conducted various training sessions as a part of our
Shepherd meetings which generally are every other

month. (The training sessions take the place of a called Shepherd's meeting.) I see part of my role within the church as an equipper (Ephesians 4:11-14). Therefore, training Shepherds is part of my responsibility.[9] As the church shifts in emphasis from professionalism to participation, there will be more widespread functioning by the church membership in areas which once were the responsibility of paid staff members.[10] Training for these tasks is, therefore, essential.

The main focus of my training to Shepherds is communication skills. My presupposition is that Shepherding is effected through communication. Healing, guiding, and sustaining are only really meaningful through relationship. Listening and sharing are, therefore, important. Various exercises are used to teach this. Usually small groups or pairs are utilized to maximize participation and advocate personal involvement. Some of the exercises are included in Appendix III.

(13) Supervision

The old saying, "It is a poor job without a good supervisor," has a lot of truth for Shepherding ministry. The manner in which our program was organized provides supervision from two areas: the elders and the minister. As I perceived our workings, the following depicts how this supervision worked. By design the oversight is not overly structured.

(A) Elders
   (1) By being Shepherds to the Shepherds as previously described.
   (2) Checking with the Shepherds to see if they are doing their job or need assistance.
   (3) Discussion about the Shepherds at elders' meeting.

  (4) By attending and participating in the Shepherd meetings and seminars.

(B) Minister

  (1) Scheduling and conducting Shepherd meetings and seminars.

  (2) Setting up individual appointments with each Shepherd.

The purpose of these appointments was to ascertain how the Shepherd was functioning, to solicit his suggestions for the program, and to discuss the families on the list. Without either of us sharing confidentialities, the purpose in talking about families was that I may know something about the people which would aid him in ministry and the Shepherd may know information which could help me.

The impetus for this procedure was the embarrassment of one Shepherd unawaringly calling on a couple going through divorce proceedings. To save future awkwardness, these sharing times were set up. When a call was then made, knowledge about "sticky" situations was known. Ministry would, therefore, be enhanced.

Most of the communication goes through the church office. The church secretary would either phone or write[11] the elders and Shepherds according to the occasion.

To keep the "ball rolling," this supervision is very necessary. Unfortunately, I have been the main ramrod of this supervision. The reasons can probably be seen in the "Evaluation" section. Good supervision will result in good ministry. Ours has been fair. The elders and myself merely supervise as individuals to individuals. The Board, nor anyone else, does not formally control the program. There is no church "legislation" concerning the Shepherding Program.

ROLE OF THE PASTOR

In light of the priesthood concept and the utilization of Shepherds, one may wonder where the pastor fits into the scope of the program's functioning. This question is valid and deserves serious attention. My intention in laying the foundation previously discussed is not to minimize, eliminate, or berate the professional ministry. The church needs full-time leadership.[12] The Scriptures justify a full-time "paid" ministry (I Corinthians 9:7-12). All within the church are to work together. The pastor and Shepherds (in fact, the whole church) are to work and to function as a team, a family, one body. The ministry intended by the Shepherding Model is a "both-and" situation, not an "either-or" situation. The total clergy of the church is essential.

In a sense, the pastor becomes a player-coach. Sometimes he carries the ball himself and other times sees that another carries it.[13] He is not merely to tell others what to do or to do it all. The pastor is a participating equipper. A balance is necessary. I have attempted to keep that balance.

Jesus' example of leadership is evident in the feeding of the five thousand. The situation necessitated an organizing of the scattered multitude in order to distribute the bread and fish in a methodical manner. Jesus could have raised His voice and shouted the commands. Rather, He directed the Apostles to seat the people on the grass in groups of hundreds and fifties (Mark 6:39,40).[14] Management[15] is the alternative to tyranny. Organization is necessary to avoid chaos.[16] Jesus chose orderliness and maximum utilization of available helpers. The pastor is an enabler, and his team is as large as his congregation.

I have learned through experience that the pastor is a key person. He can keep the people merely as members on a church roll or he can make them member-ministers.[17] Most plans of pastoral ministry by laymen depend upon the minister for impetus and direction.[18] This reality has often frustrated me, for I have thought more leadership should come from within the church. Upon contemplation, however, this lacking of initiative and follow-through may very well be the result of failure[19] on my part and previous ministers to adequately train the leaders (or even the whole church).

This failure makes the training program as vital as preaching. Training should be done for specific ministries,[20] hospital calling, death calling, reclaiming inactive members and the such. The training should be a practical apprenticeship. The minister is a multiplier. If the Shepherds are reached with a new vision of the church, others can consequently be reached through them.[21] The minister is to develop people for Christ's service in the church. In a sense he is the head of a seminary, a training school for workers.[22]

The pastor is important, not because he is wiser or better than other persons, but because he is in a position to draw out, to develop, and to direct the powers of other people. In strengthening these already committed Shepherds, the first task is to teach. It is significant that Ephesians 4:12[23] equates pastor to teacher.[24] As a teacher he teaches others to teach (II Timothy 2:2). He is to inspire, to moderate, and to animate the congregation. He may be authoritative, but not authoritarian.[25] I have tried to fit this role.

Some, and even myself at times, fear letting people minister in very vital and often fragile situations. One must trust God and God's people for the handling of such situations.

In speaking about training nationals on the mission field, Melvin Hodges makes a significant point which can apply to Shepherding. "If we insist that men must be fully capable before we trust them with responsibility, we shall never be ready to let go of the reins of government."[26] Many pastors are about the work of the ministry as the mother who told her daughter, "Don't go near the water till you learn how to swim."

This kind of total ministry by the pastor results in definite pay-offs. As the pastor clarifies his role and expresses his skills, competencies, preferences, and goals, most congregations respond affirmatively. The pastor cannot do all things and do them all well. How well I have learned! By trying to do everything, the pastor may well foster confusion.[27] Furthermore, Southard makes this significant statement:

> Lay ministeries grow as clergy become resource persons rather than task-oriented managers, and lay leaders provide support for the clergyperson as a coach and accept pastoral responsibilities.[28]

The more the Shepherds and I work as a team, the more affirmation and ministry will be performed. It makes no difference who does the work if the glory is God's.[29]

In concluding this section, may it be noted that the fundamental principle is that biblical leadership by the pastor is to equip the whole flock for ministry. The example of Jesus is to be followed here as expressed in Hebrews 13:20,21, "Lord Jesus, that Great Shepherd of the sheep, equip you with everything good for doing His will."[30] The ministry is mutual in Shepherding. The "laity" are looking for compassionate and competent leadership; hopefully, the pastor can provide that. By the same token, the pastor is searching for committed and talented laity.[31] The Shepherding program, as I have experienced it, is an attempt in that area.

The minister as equipper becomes a catalyst, model, coordinator, and visionary. The area I have not developed efficiently, but hope to improve on, is modeling. Paul mentioned modeling in I Thessalonians 1:6 when he wrote, "You also became imitators of us." The word "imitate" is literally "to mimic." The Thessalonians learned by Paul's modeling. They watched him and learned to minister by his example.

Ministry is taught, but it is also caught. Jesus instructed His followers formally, but He also taught them by example. He made disciples of them by living among them and showing them how to minister. To transfer that concept to Shepherding, I believe I should encourage my elders, deacons, and Shepherds to sit in on counseling sessions, go to the hospital and homes on calls, assist in funeral arrangements, and share with me in other areas of ministry. The job description could be taken and modeled for the Shepherds. This on-the-job training or "discipling" through modeling ministry may very well be the key to more vital Shepherding! I have not done much of this. I have, however, tried to teach and to motivate the people to vital ministry.

The fact that many persons can do most of what a pastor does can be very threatening. The special task of the pastor is to prepare for service and to support them through administration and example in that service.[32] The healing profession, ministry included, is to assist people toward interdependence rather than dependence.[33] The ministerial office is not a special privilege but rather a practical responsibility.[34] The ministry and growth is, therefore, expanded and multiplied.

SUMMARY

The development of Shepherds is very significant to the success of the program. This development is based upon the presupposition of the Priesthood of Believers. This belief justifies the enlistment (by general and personal call), the training (for competency and confidence in ministry), and the supervision (for assistance and accountability) of Shepherds based upon an agreed job description. Such clarification assists communication and ownership of the program. Through this process my role as pastor is becoming exceedingly clearer to myself and the congregation. Hopefully, this clarification is creating mutual affirmation and multiplying the ministry performed.

NOTES

[1]Eugene Stowe, *The Ministry of Shepherding* (Kansas City, Missouri:Q Beacon Hill Press, 1976), p. 89.

[2]Jay E. Adams in his book *Pastoral Leadership* on p. 13 states, "To each member of the flock, Christ has given gifts through His Spirit and has assigned them tasks to do that are appropriate to those gifts. He had provided leadership for the purpose of helping every sheep discover, develop and deploy his gifts in ways that contribute to the welfare of the entire flock and that further His purpose in this world." It is clear, therefore, that all leadership in the church is functional.

[3]Adams, *Pastoral Leadership*, p. 87.

[4]Stowe, *Ministry of Shepherding*, p. 15.

[5]I have not always succeeded in this area. There are also other personal factors which arise causing Shepherds not to fulfill the expectations, e.g. too many irons in the fire.

[6]Feucht, *Everyone A Minister*, p. 109.

[7]Lyle Schaller, *The Decision-Makers* (Nashville: Abingdon, 1974), p. 67.

[8]Jay Adams in his book *Pastoral Leadership* on p. 86 takes the following very directive approach. I have not totally followed his advice, but include it as thought provoking. "Instead, after testing several likely persons in other or in similar tasks (have them teach for a period every now and then as a substitute, etc.), and after agreement by the members of the board of elders, the person chosen should be appointed to the

task, then told so by the pastor and/or another elder. He should not be asked if he will serve, but rather be told that he is the man (woman) that they want for this task. While reasonable cause for declination should be honored (the man truly does not have time now to do this because of certain previously unknown family matters), if less weighty reasons are adduced, the pastor should press the appointment by challenging him to enter into the opportunity (which should be spelled out specifically along with the obligations and duties involved) and stress the need of the whole body for his ministry. Unless truly weighty reasons are forthcoming, the pastor should refuse to take no for an answer."

[9]Stowe, *The Ministry of Shepherding,* p. 132.

[10]Lyle Schaller, *The Pastor and The People* (Nashville: Abingdon Press, 1973), p. 23.

[11]Three such letters are found in Appendix IV.

[12]Paul Benjamin in *The Growing Congregation* on page 25 states, "It would be wrong, however, to assume that God's people are to function without leadership. From the sociologist's viewpoint, no group can continue without leadership."

[13] Trueblood, *The Incendiary Fellowship,* p. 43. Findley Edge agrees with this concept as seen in his book *The Greening of the Church* on page 43.

[14]Stowe, *The Ministry of Shepherding,* p. 132.

[15]A practical demonstration of the importance of this phase of shepherding was shown in a time study conducted with a large group of pastors. The result showed that 25 per cent of the average pastor's week was spent in the preaching-teaching area and 25 per cent in pastoral care activities, but 50 per cent of this time was spent in administration or management responsibilities. Nathan M. Pusey, and Charles L. Taylor, *Ministry for Tomorrow* (New York: Seabury Press, 1967), p. 38.

[16]Peter Drucker, *Management* (New York: Harper & Row, 1974), pp. 3-10.

[17]Feucht, *Everyone a Minister,* p. 99.

[18]Shedd, *Pastoral Ministry of Church Officers,* p. 20.

[19]A statement on reasons for failure by Jay Adams are found at the end of this work.

[20]Feucht, *Everyone a Minister,* p. 101.

[21]Trueblood, *The Incendiary Fellowship,* p. 35.

[22]Feucht, *Everyone a Minister,* p. 96.

[23]Paul Benjamin in *The Growing Congregation on page 28 writes, "In the 4th chapter of Ephesians, the apostle Paul leaves very little doubt about the primary role of those who function as leaders in the Body of Christ. They are to equip the saints for ministry (vs. 11). Unfortunately, many translations have a comma which separates 'saints' from 'the work of the ministry'. This misplaced punctuation has sometimes been referred to as the 'fatal comma'. Leaving out the comma, the passage reads, 'And His gifts were that some should be apostles, some prophets, some evangelists, some pastors and teachers, FOR EQUIPPING OF THE SAINTS FOR THE WORK OF THE MINISTRY. . . ' The work of Christian leadership is then clearly defined as preparing the people of God to minister."*

[24]Trueblood, The Incendiary Fellowship, pp. 36, 43, 44.

[25]Feucht, *Everyone a Minister*, p. 51.

[26]Melvin Hodges, *The Indigenous Church* (Springfield, Missouri: Gospel Publishing House, 1953), p. 31.

[27]Biersdorf, *Creating an Intentional Ministry*, pp. 21, 22.

[28]Southard, *Comprehensive Pastoral Care*, pp. 63, 64.

[29]Robert Girard, *Brethren, Hang Loose* (Grand Rapids: Zondervan, 1972), p. 43.

[30]Adams, *Pastoral Leadership*, p. 23.

[31]Calian, *Today's Pastor*, p. 37. Calian does an excellent job of tracing historically the relationship of clergy and laity on pages 66-70. His view is that clergy leadership will still exist even if the Priesthood of Believers becomes a reality. I agree.

[32]Samuel Calian in *Today's Pastor in Tomorrow's World* on pages 82, 83 profoundly writes, "If the leadership of the laity is to be truly realized, pastors will need to give careful attention to the following steps: (1) A higher grade of theological education should be provided for the laity. (2) Pastors should have a guiding motto never to do a task for which a layperson is better qualified (produces ownership in the church). (3) Pastors who wish to avoid the pitfalls of being either a superstar or a fallen messiah within the parish should educate the congregation from the beginning that the church belongs to the people. (4) Pastors, who are tuned to needs of the marketplace, will encourage qualified persons among the laity and minister meaningfully to these needs."

[33]Southard, *Comprehensive Pastoral Care*, pp. 7, 8.

[34]Stowe, *Ministry of Shepherding*, p. 30.

CHAPTER V

Evaluation

"If we could first know where we are, and whither we are tending,
we could better judge what to do and how to do it."
Abraham Lincoln

EXPLANATION

The evaluation process is very important because it affords the opportunity to search-the-soul of the program. The evaluations have helped me to think through the program and to attempt to make changes where appropriate. In developing an evaluation process I have come at it from four angles. The first and foremost is the congregation. They are the persons ministered to; therefore, their voice should be the most significant. If anyone can determine the effectiveness of a program, it is the people whom the program is to effect. Their input came through an evaluation questionnaire and an at-random telephone survey.

Secondly, the Shepherds evaluate the program through verbal interchanges at the meetings and by means of the questionnaire used by the congregation. Againn their insight is valuable, for they are putting the program into action. The Shepherds, therefore, generally know what will and will not work.

The third source is pastors from the area. I presented our program to these pastors and a committee from their congregations. Their feedback is helpful, for often a person not actively involved in something can be more objective in his assessment. Furthermore, by not knowing about the program, they often asked questions that I or our people did not ask. These additional questions assist in analyzing the situation.

Finally, I evaluate the program from my perspective of its strengths and weaknesses. My conclusions about these evaluations are found in the last chapter. Hopefully, this process agrees with Lyle Schaller when he states, "The simplest system of accountability is one in which the sources of funding, the clientele, and the policy-makers are all represented in one group."[1]

CONGREGATION

In determining a method for evaluation, the Shepherds compiled a questionnaire. Their view was to keep it short and simple with the hope of more people participating. The following form is what they drew up.

CONGREGATION EVALUATION OF SHEPHERDING PROGRAM

CENTRAL CHRISTIAN CHURCH

BELOIT, WISCONSIN

I. What do you feel the Shepherding Program is?............................

....

II. What would you list as qualifications for a Shepherd?................

....

III. Has your Shepherd met these (or your) qualification?.................

....

PLEASE CHECK ANSWERS YOU CONSIDER APPROPRIATE

IV. You would expect your Shepherd to contact you when:

    A. You are in morning worship

    B. The church must relay information to you

    C. You are in the hospital

    D. You have been absent for 6-8 weeks

    E. There has been a death in the family

    F. Other Suggestions:...

V. You would expect to contact your Shepherd when:

    A. You desire assistance with a problem

    B. Other: ....

VI. The Shepherding Program is a valuable function in the church:

    A. Yes ....

    B. ....

VII. In what way can the church strengthen its Shepherding Program

....

....

....

Sign if desired

This evaluation sheet was distributed in the Fall of 1976 and the Spring of 1978. The Shepherds gave the questionnaire to their people; but most of them, contrary to my wish, did not pick them up or make definite arrangements for the office to receive them. I believe that this procedure helps to account for the small number returned. (Only about twenty per cent of the congregation responded. This is in contrast to the great number of talent survey sheets returned when the personal collection was utilized.)

Upon receiving these evaluations, I asked some assistance in tabulating the results. I chose two very competent women for this task, both of whom were previous secretaries at the church. Here are the results of those tabulations.

Congregation Evaluation of Shepherding Program (Forty total responses. September 1976)

I. *What do you feel the Shepherding Program is?*

Thirteen people felt that it was a program of Christian concern. Twelve felt that it was having someone to call on in time of need, someone other than the minister to turn to for help. Ten felt that it was a program of caring or concern by the church. Eight felt that it involved a fellowship of the members of the congregation. Seven people believed that it provided someone to talk to. Four felt that it included getting to know others in the church better, and three only stated that it was a good program.

Several did not reply; perhaps they still do not fully understand the Shepherding program and, therefore, would not be using it. Perhaps they are the ones who need it the most.

It seemed that most felt it was someone who would be concerned about them, would care about their problems, someone to talk to, Christian fellowship.

II. *What should you list as qualifications of a Shepherd?*

Fifteen people felt that the main qualification of a Shepherd should be caring for other people, concerned with others. Thirteen also listed being kind, understanding, and thoughtful as qualifications. Eleven people felt that a Shepherd should be a Christian, friendly, and willing to be a Shepherd. Eight felt that they should be interested in people, and four felt that they should be active in the church.

It seemed that most felt the Shepherd must have a great deal of concern for others, not be superficial, but a true understanding, have a genuine liking for people, not be pushy, hold confidences as strictly confidential, someone to talk to, a friend.

III. *Has your Shepherd met these (or your) qualifications?*

Twenty-nine responded that they definitely felt that their Shepherd had met the qualifications. Two felt that their Shepherd had not met the qualifications, and two were indifferent. There were no really definite "bad" comments. Many commented that their own particular Shepherd had gone above and beyond the call of duty in their services.

IV. *You would expect your Shepherd to contact you when:*

A. *In morning worship.*

Thirteen felt this would be nice; most seemed to feel other times were more important.

B. *When the church must relay information.*

Fourteen felt that this would be a time for Shepherd contact. Many indicated that we have the "Evangel" and bulletin for this purpose, but it would be helpful in special situations.

C. *You are in the hospital.*

Thirty people felt that they would expect a contact from their Shepherd during a hospitalization.

D. *When you have been absent for six to eight weeks.*

Twenty-eight felt you should be contacted after this much absence. Several commented that this was too long a period; one should be contacted after two to three weeks except in special situations (vacations, etc.).

E. *When there has been a death in the family.*

This was almost unanimous. Thirty-two felt that a contact at these times was essential.

F. *Other suggestions.*

Special occasions such as golden anniversaries or other happy occasions. Some felt that in lieu of a personal visit, a telephone call would be appropriate, just to keep in contact.

V. *You would expect to contact your Shepherd when:*

Twenty-three people responded that they would expect to contact their Shepherd when they felt they needed help with a problem or other special situations such as a stress in the family, divorce, family problems, problems with children, etc. Several indicated they would contact their Shepherd when they "just needed to talk." It was also noted that it is necessary for the member to contact the Shepherd at times like these the Shepherd is willing to help but often does not know of the situation. Shepherd are not mind-readers.

VI. *The Shepherding Program is a valuable function of the church.*

Thirty-three people felt that the program was worthwhile, three felt that it was of no value, and two really did not know. One commented that the church circles were doing an adequate job and could take the place of the Shepherds but felt it is a good program for widows or others who are alone.

VII. *In what way can the church strengthen its Shepherding Program?*

There were several suggestions for improvement, many of which seemed to come from the Shepherds themselves. They felt there should be more Shepherd meetings, more opportunities to discuss the problems that they are facing, more seminars, and a desire for the members to contact them if a problem does arise. The members felt that they should not hesitate to contact a Shepherd, that a Shepherd should be willing to be a Shepherd and if not functioning properly, should be replaced.

Many commented that it is an excellent program and felt that it was functioning adequately at the present time.

Congregational Responses on Evaluation of Shepherding Program
(Thirty-two responses. April 1978)

I. *What do you feel the Shepherding Program is?*

One person left this blank; one said, "I don't know"; and one felt the program was unnecessary. Other responses included such things as communication and caring, contact with church members and attenders, an effort to reach members to encourage attendance, a concerned friend through the church, a program for people to work and fellowship together, keeping God's children closer together and in touch with anyone needing help, support for the minister, someone to contact when you need spiritual guidance, interested help, promotion of spiritual growth, people setting a Christian example or other member, and a way to bring people together to get better acquainted.

II. *What would you list as qualifications for a Shepherd?*

Five did not answer this. Seven specifically stated the Shepherd should be a Christian. Other attributes listed included: loving, caring for people, kind, interest in the church, willing and physically able to get around, faithful in attendance, friendly without being pushy, helpful, compassionate, understanding, helping others, willing to work, concern for fellow Christians, sympathetic, wants to put the Lord's work first, happy and cheerful, pleasant, strong faith, and have a knowledge of the Bible.

III. *Has your Shepherd met these (or your) qualifications?*

Eighteen said yes, five left it blank, and nine had vague responses.

IV. *You would expect your Shepherd to contact you when:*

A. *You are in morning worship* - 6.

B. *The church must relay information to you* - 10. (The church paper was specified by one as a means of relaying information.)

C. *You are in the hospital* - 27.

D. *You have been absent for six to eight weeks* - 23. (Someone felt three to six weeks was more desirable.)

E. *There has been a death in the family* - 27.

F. Other: Items mentioned included happy occasions such as graduations, anniversaries, etc. Another thought when the Shepherd felt a contact was necessary, and another said when there is a specific need in the church. One specifically stated not to wait for sickness or death to visit, and another felt phone calls sometimes would be welcome.

V. *You would expect to contact your Shepherd when:*

A. *You desire assistance with a problem.*

Twenty-three responses. One stipulated the sheep must first try to solve the problem alone before calling the Shepherd, realizing some people might overdo and "abuse" the Shepherd. Another made a point of letting the Shepherd know of the problem, as the Shepherd is not a mind reader. Another specified they would prefer the minister for help with problems.

Other: One felt he would contact the Shepherd to inquire about a church activity. Another would contact the Shepherd to learn of procedure on funerals and weddings. Two people felt it was a two-way street in that the sheep should contact the Shepherd when the Shepherd was ill or in the hospital or when the sheep knew the Shepherd had a problem. Another mentioned contacting the Shepherd in times of sickness or death, as he might not have heard.

VI. *The Shepherd Program is a valuable function in the church.*

A. *Yes* - 28.

B. *No* - 1. (One felt the minister or assistant minister could perform the same functions.)

Blank - 2.

VII. *In what way can the church strengthen its Shepherding Program?*

One said, "no suggestions"; eighteen people left it blank. Other comments suggested meetings, communications, fellowship, more calls, concern, to remind people they have a Shepherd to call if a need arises, continuing training sessions, qualified Shepherds, team training as a means of Shepherd training, keeping the church members aware of the program, choosing people to serve who like people and have the time to serve, and changing the Shepherd if the "sheep" is not comfortable with the assigned Shepherd.

Not being fully satisfied with the above process, the elders and I tried another means of congregational response. One of the focuses of the program is to reactivate inactive members. On every Shepherd list there are at least one or two families in this category. These people in most likelihood did not respond to the questionnaire. Therefore, two families from each Shepherd's care were listed who were considered "fringe area" in their church activity. Then in an at-random telephone survey, eight of these families were called on the phone. They were asked the following questions:

(1) Has your Shepherd contacted you?
(2) Has it made any difference to you?
(3) What do you think of the Shepherd Program?
No names will be mentioned. These are their responses:

Telephone Survey of Shepherding Program
Spring 1977

A.
   1. No
   2. No
   3. None

B.
   1. No
   2. No
   3. Good idea — if run right

C.
1. Not since Christmas
2. Yes — Prays with me
3. OK — should have had it a long time ago

D.
1. No — probably because my phone is unlisted and I work three jobs (talked to her in church)
2. No — it was never explained fully to me
3. Good idea for some, but I prefer direct contact with the minister

E.
1. No
2. No
3. Don't know nothing about it

F.
1. Yes, but rather she didn't
2. No
3. Rather see the minister

G.
1. Yes
2. Haven't been too active since wife died
3. Don't know too much about it

H.
1. Yes
2. Yes
3. Really helps a lot of people

Telephone Survey of Shepherding Program
Summer 1978

A.
1. Yes
2. No
3. Good

B.
1. No — probably because we are hardly ever home
2. No
3. It certainly can't be doing any harm

C.
1. No
2. No difference
3. I think it's OK. Don't know too much about it

D.
1. No
2. No
3. I think it's a good idea

E.
1. Yes
2. Yes
3. Very good program

F.
1. Yes
2. No
3. From a personal experience it hasn't done anything for me, because I haven't needed anything. Probably would use it if had to.

G.
1. Yes
2. Yes
3. Good program. It would be great if it worked properly. Personally it came at a time when I needed it.

H.(Former Shepherd)
1. Yes, a great deal of contact
2. No
3. Should have a Shepherd that is really compatible with you. Good program when working.

I.(New member)
1. Yes
2. No
3. Both parties must work together

Summary: S-Spring
1. Five answered no (one said not since Christmas and one said her phone has an unlisted number).
Three answered yes (and one said yes but rather she didn't).

2. Five answered no; two answered yes; one commented that he hasn't been too active since his wife died.

3. Three answered — Do not know anything about it. Two thought it was a good idea. Two preferred seeing the minister. One stated that it really helps a lot of people.

Summary: Spring 1978

1. Three answered no; six answered yes (one was very emphatic)
2. Seven answered no; two answered yes.
3. All but one viewed the program as meaningful and helpful. This one did not know much about the program.

SHEPHERDS

During a regular meeting in the Spring of 1978, twelve Shepherds were asked to fill out evaluation forms. Here are the results.

Shepherds Evaluation of Shepherding Program (Twelve responses. Spring 1978)

I. *What do you feel the Shepherding Program is?*

Answers included such remarks as contact with members, a bridge of friendship and concern, a program to build attendance and spiritual growth, a way to reach each person in the church, a way to know you can call on someone in the church before going to the preacher, and a function to draw church members closer together.

II. *What would you list as qualifications for a Shepherd?*

Responses from the Shepherds themselves were fairly similar and included such things as being an active member, being a good Christian, being a person with real devotion and faithfulness, being a person with knowledge of Scriptures and of church functions, one with an interest in the members on their list, one who will pray for their sheep and have time to devote to people, being a person who is friendly, pleasant, loving, kind, considerate, thoughtful, trustworthy, dedicated, concerned, and able to keep confidences.

III. *Has your Shepherd met these (or your) qualifications?*

Five people left this blank. Five people responded yes. Two answers were vague as to a definite yes or no.

IV. *Would you expect your Shepherd to contact you when:*

A. *You are in morning worship* - Six answered yes.

B. *The church must relay information to you* - Six again answered yes.

C. *You are in the hospital* - All twelve answered yes.

D. *You have been absent for six to eight weeks* - Ten answered yes.

E. *There has been a death in the family* - All twelve answered yes.

F. *Other* - Answers included birthdays, prayer, and any time when the Shepherd can be of help.

V. *You would want to contact your Shepherd when:*

A. *You desire assistance with a problem* - Six answered yes.

B. *Other* - Responses included when you are lonely, ill, or need assistance.

VI. *The Shepherding Program is a valuable function of the church:*

A. *Yes* - All twelve Shepherds answered yes.

B. *No* - None.

VII. *In what way can the church strengthen its Shepherding Program?*

Responses included remarks such as to make more calls, to follow the program as it is outlined, to work harder to make people aware of the program, to encourage proper priorities, and to elicit more dedication on the part of the Shepherds.

As would be expected,[2] the Shepherds have been positive in their responses to the program. Although we have had a change-over of several Shepherds for personal reasons, only one had serious questions about the program's validity. This person apparently did not agree with our procedure of evaluating the program. When asked at the meetings about their views, the unanimous judgment is that Shepherding is very significant, worthwhile, and important in the life of the church. The main regret is that most do not feel they are doing justice to the program or ministering adequately. Hopefully, this feeling can be alleviated through further training and affirmation by myself, fellow Shepherds, and the congregation. It should be noted that at the Shepherd meetings support is given to each other through identification of similar problems faced and suggestions as to how to solve these problems.

AREA PASTORS

The following pastors have been gracious enough to submit their evaluation of our program in light of what they hope to do in their congregations. All of these churches have adopted our program and adapted it to their specific needs. Dr. Richard Boyer is minister of the United Methodist Church in Roscoe, Illinois. David Kinnick is senior minister of the Church of Christ in Footville, Wisconsin. Furthermore, Phyllis Peterson and Bill Ryerson of the Grace Lutheran Church of Loves Park, Illinois, have also initiated this program in their congregation.

Dear Joe,

The mechanics of the shepherding program are excellent. We have used the model as it exists in your church. It has been helpful, inspirational, and a practical guide. It has been a way to spread out the caring of our church members to more workers. This has filled a real void in our church.

We have had problems similar to yours in securing enough shepherds to do the task, and having a few who have not functioned adequately. A part of our evaluation has been a confession and forgiveness of one another in the tasks we have failed at as shepherds (mostly sins of omission).

I see three tensions that the shepherding program has created in our church, which we struggle with. I think they are inevitable.

(1) Some of our shepherds are spread too thin in their services to the church. They are capable of shepherding, but other ministries compete for their time.

(2) Evangelistic outreach to new persons has slowed down, a ministry that is so needed in our growing community. We cannot have very many shepherds doing double calling duty, and we will have to recruit and train a whole new visitation team for evangelism. This is not an easy task.

(3) There is a tension between caring for our own and for confronting the world. There is a desire on the part of many to become "ingrown." The shepherding, which is so vital, can become a force which supports the "ingrown" nature of our fellowship. We must constantly battle that trend. With all of the above tensions, shepherding is still well worth doing, and I hope it continues in our congregation.

Sincerely,

Dick Boyer

An Evaluation of the Shepherding Program used by Central Christian Church, Beloit, Wisconsin. Joe Grana, Minister.

This evaluation is based upon careful study of the materials pertinent to the "Shepherding Program." In addition to the printed material, two personal presentations of the program by Joe Grana have been most helpful.

The program is well documented in its scriptural rationale and also in its contemporary need. I have noticed some people seem to identify "shepherding" with "elders," so perhaps a title expressive of care and concern, but without the use of the word shepherd, would present one less barrier to some people.

The strong points of the program seem to be in the fellowship it fosters; i.e. (1) training sessions, (2) bi-monthly or quarterly meetings of shepherds, (3) the involvements of the elders in overseeing, (4) and certainly the fellowship between shepherds and the flock.

The job description is also very concise, but not cumbersome. To use it in our local situation, we will be making some minor changes, but we see the program as very beneficial, and hope to cultivate our people to care and show concern as a normal function of the Christian life. This program, to be totally effective, will help lead our people to "shepherd" to such an extent that a program is no longer needed.

We are pleased to have this program shared with us and we look forward to using it.

In His Service,

David Kinnick

Dear Joe:

I don't know if this is what you were hoping for or not, but what a story I have to tell you.

A beautiful thing is happening in our church . . . the Grace Lutheran Church of Loves Park. On February 4th we had our first meeting concerning the beginning of the Shepherding Program you developed. We were but a handful of people who were sincere in our hopes to begin an outreach program that would be effective in caring for the needs of the members of our church . . . especially those who might be forgotten and neglected. That was three months ago.

How could it be that in just three short months this would turn out to be so enthusiastically accepted by so many people?

We're finding people have a real need to touch the lives of others in our congregation and the Shepherding Program is their opportunity to channel those desires . . . and to release the deep need of sharing the blessings God has bestowed upon them. More than that, they're so thankful that your Shepherding Program is pointing the way!

It's truly making us feel like a flock! No one expected the flood of members who volunteered to be shepherds! No one expected the ease with which these wonderful people would assume their responsibilities. Some of them even fell into the job. One woman was called to be asked if she would like to be a shepherd. She said no . . . explained that her husband had just entered the hospital and that she could sure use a shepherd right now. He was able to minister to her needs immediately.

We have found the 30 Minute taped interview that closely follows the outline you gave us is one of the most valuable tools we have. Everyone who has listened to the tape has become a zone leader or a shepherd. This interview has been dubbed several times over. Each zone leader has it and is using it for recruitment purposes, as well as refreshing the memory . . . plus leading and teaching our present shepherds.

There are over 1500 members in our church (probably the 2nd or 3rd largest Lutheran church in the Rockford-Loves Park area). We are overwhelmed that 75 percent of our members now have shepherds . . . in **only** 3 months! That's an accomplishment in itself!

Not a day goes by that people don't call to tell us they would like to be shepherds or work in some capacity.

It's exciting . . . it's one of the most important programs to happen in our church. It's bringing about a unification we never realized was possible before and we're grateful to your work for that.

Last Monday, April 21st, we had our first joint meeting with zone leaders and shepherds. It was on a circle night and we thought it would have a poor turnout because of the competition. However, Founder's Hall was filled to capacity. Pastor Smith had a look of incredulity on his face. He said he has often thought "Oh ye of little faith" when listening to others doubt, but this time he had to say it to himself.

Everyone involved is enthusiastic about our shepherding program and we look forward to giving you a report 6 months to a year from now when we evaluate how well the program is working.

Until then, thank you for sharing your efforts with us. Many people will benefit from it, and we know its value will be proven in the future!

Through Christ's love,

Phyllis Peterson
Bill Ryerson
Members of Grace Lutheran Church

MY EVALUATION

The judgments that I have are mixed. It is, therefore, easier for me to list the strengths and weaknesses of the program from my perspective.

Weaknesses:

(1) Not all the Shepherds are functioning properly.

(2) The elders do not yet completely oversee the program, I do.

(3) Ownership is not complete.

(4) Seminars and meetings are not as well attended as I think they should be.

Strengths:

(1) More people are now involved in ministry. (The priesthood is growing.)

(2) The concept is biblical (based on Scripture) and practical (applied through job description).

(3) The church is developing a great unity and, thus, becoming a family and body partially through this effort.

In other words, I see a lot of progress, but there is a lot to make. The difference between now and before the program began is like comparing a half loaf of bread with no loaf. The program and, therefore, the church have grown and progressed. Time will be needed for Shepherding to become an integral dimension of the church, but it is "becoming." My conviction is that the Shepherding Model of Ministry has the potential of being the most vital form of ministry within the church. The reason for such a statement is because of the unlimited possibilities of ministry it opens up.

SUMMARY

The evaluation process is a soul-searching time. It is necessary so judgments can be made as to where one has been and in what direction one will go. I believe the evaluations assisted in this and covered all the bases: Shepherds, congregation as a whole, "fringe" area people, the pastor (myself), and outside resources. Conclusions about these evaluations will be shared in the next chapter as well as some future possibilities and hopes.

NOTES

[1]Lyle Schaller, *The Decision Makers* (Nashville: Abingdon, 1974), p. 201.

[2]They probably would not be Shepherds if they did not believe in this ministry.

CHAPTER VI

Conclusions and Future Hopes

"The important thing in the world is not so much in where we are, as in which direction we are going."
Oliver Wendell Holmes

FAILURES AND SUCCESSES

Unlike Solomon's quest, the end of the matter has not been heard when it comes to the Shepherding Program. Hopefully, the above statement by Holmes is ringing true as this ministry is becoming what it could. However, not all the conclusions are positive.

Upon analyzing the evaluations, I must admit some failures in the program. The failure is not with the concept. The majority of responses were definitely favorable toward the ministry and organization of Shepherding. The failure came in the implementation. Jesus' statement to the Apostles in the Garden of Gethsemane is definitely applicable, "The Spirit is willing, but the flesh is weak." (Matthew 26:41)

The at random phoning indicated that several Shepherds had not been making their calls. Furthermore, the program had not made a significant difference in some of their lives. Conclusions about such reactions, however, are difficult to understand concretely. On the one hand, it looks like the Shepherds failed by not doing their task at all or by not doing it well. On the other hand, the Shepherds may have been unable to make contact because of scheduling conflicts and these people may not have had in their recent pasts opportunities for ministry which would make a strong impact on their lives (e.g., serious illness or death of loved ones). Another factor is that the time element often necessary for the development of intimate relationships and for a program to be a vital part of a congregation has not yet been long enough. These possibilities cannot be excuses. Failure is failure. However, analysis of the totality of an issue is necessary.

Communication is a perenniel problem with churches. Being on the "inside," one sometimes forgets how little is communicated. Even though the newsletter, bulletin, pulpit, and calls by the Shepherds were utilized, more advertisement and information could always be done.

The failures, therefore, resulted in shortcomings by myself, the elders, and the Shepherds. Administration, oversight, communications, and implementation were the culprits. However, being an eternal optimist, I am not discouraged.

As I view some of the Shepherds, I have seen exciting growth in their capacity to minister. Their insights and activities into pastoral care have caused them to be endeared by the rest of the community of faith. These Shepherds have been very conscientious in their contacts and have been appreciated in their ministry. Their assistance has greatly alleviated my work load. I can call on them to help and am assured that the job will be well done. More members of the church are being consistently called on than ever before. In my opinion, this can only strengthen the church. The elders, in this regard, are also very reliable.

As the evaluations do indicate, some vital ministry has resulted from the ministry of this program. The majority of the people responding did so in a very positive manner. This amount of ministry is certainly better than no ministry. Therefore, if some are working, it is better than the "none" in this capacity previously. I believe more is being done than is actually known. I look for this ministry to grow as time passes. The numbers and quality of ministry will expand in my estimation. I believe in the concept and its scriptural undergirding. We are "becoming." I hope others will too. As Holmes has stated, the direction we are going is the important factor.

FUTURE GOALS

For various reasons, the following possible off-shoots of this program have not been started at Beloit. They are, however, possibilities for the future and could be utilized by other congregations as they begin their ministry.

    (1) Become sharing groups through monthly fellowship suppers and times of expression and prayer.

    (2) Conduct Bible studies at the various members' homes.

    (3) Call on church visitors in their area.

    (4) Become an evangelistic arm of the church through calling on, inviting, and teaching those outside the church.

    (5) Activate community social action in their areas.

CONCLUSIONS

From my perspective, the organization and concept of the Shepherding Program is good and worthwhile. The only exception would be the necessity of dividing everyone geographically. In some ways this has been helpful; but, as time has passed, its usage has been laid aside. Due to present mobility, distance is not much of a problem. More important is

Shepherd-flock match-up. An idea that may come to fruition would be matching some Shepherds with their "clientele" (e.g., college age, widowed, divorced). However, the present form is adequate.

This program has been a rewarding element in my life. There have been frustrations with the shortcomings, but the blessings of this ministry have brought a balance. I believe the effects of this ministry have increased the cohesiveness of the fellowship and family atmosphere of the congregation. My excitement is increased as other congregations have adapted our program and others may also do so.

Unto the "Great Shepherd" may honor and glory and dominion be given for the ministry of healing He has exemplified.

OTHER SCRIPTURES ON PRIESTHOOD OF BELIEVERS

Matthew 16:16-19; 18:18

Luther shows that Christ did not give his keys to Peter and his successors personally, but to the whole church and congregation. . . . We would not overlook the fact that when Jesus refers to the keys he used the plural form . . . Luther's view is that the word is not received through ordination but through a call to service, and if ordination does not take place, it is not integral to the ministry independently of ordination. It follows that ordination is only a public confirmation of calling, and what is received in calling is not some special gift of grace or power by a commission.[1]

I Corinthians 4

For although we are all equally priests, still not all of us can serve a ministry and preach. Thus St. Paul says in I Corinthians 4: "We do not desire to be held by the people and be other than servants of Christ and stewards of the Gospel".[2]

Ephesians 4:16

"The body will build itself up in love, as each part does its work" (Ephesians 4:16). There is no place for spectators in the body of Christ. Just as every part of the human body must operate properly for effective function, so every believer must do his part. Everyone is needed and is important.[3]

Titus 2:14

In his letter to Titus Paul speaks of Christ "who gave Himself for us to redeem us from all iniquity and to purify for himself a people of his own who are zealous for good deeds."[4]

Hebrews 13:15

Let it be observed, therefore, that the whole church is being exhorted to offer this sacrifice of praise. If the sacrifice of the mass should here be meant, then everyone in the church must be a mass priest.[5]

MARKS OF A ROYAL PRIESTHOOD

(1) Baptism   Romans 1:5,6; I John 2:2;; Titus 3:4-7; John 3:5

(2) Sacrifice   Revelation 1:56; *Martus* - Martyr, witness. Be faithful unto death. I Peter 2:5; Romans 11:30-33.

(3) Worship   Romans 12:1,2. Use of *Latreia* - "worship" designates priests here for that term was used of priests and service people. The term *Latreuein* - "worship" is used of the twelve tribes of Israel.[6]

LUTHER'S VIEW OF THE TRUE CHURCH

Luther states that there are seven outward marks by which the true church may be known. These are:

(1) The preaching of the word.

(2) The Sacrament of Baptism.

(3) The Sacrament of the Lord's Supper.

(4) The keys of Christian discipline and forgiveness.

(5) A called and consecrated Christian ministry.

(6) Public worship, with prayers, praise, and thanksgiving.

(7) The Holy Cross: i.e., suffering in many forms through which the church must inevitably pass. To begin by an imitation of Christ and then proceed to faith, is a common error. The right order is to start in faith and proceed to love, i.e., to that kind of service which cannot be dissociated from the cross. The Christian begins in faith, develops in love, and this love involves suffering. It means carrying the cross.[7]

DENOMINATIONAL VIEWS OF PRIESTHOOD
Methodism:

A look at two Wesley hymns in his 1739 edition demonstrates the attitude espoused:

#642
O That all were taught of God,
All annointed by Thy Grace,
Kings and priests redeemed with Blood,
Born again to sound Thy praise.

#16
O what an age of golden days!
O what a choice pecular race!
Washed in the Lamb's all-cleansing Blood,
Anointed Kings and Priests to God.[8]

Eastwood demonstrates from the writings of Wesley and the Methodist Church that they believe the Holy Spirit is given to all Christians to fulfill a definite ministry. The possession of a gift implies a debt to others in the form of ministry. All Christians are viewed a priests through regeneration.
Congregationalists:

The gifts of ministry and the orders and offices in the church are given not to individuals to exercise in the church, but to the church to be exercised by individuals . . . in Congregationalism it is the whole church which celebrates the Sacraments and offers worship. It is at this point that the words of I Peter are applied to the whole church, we are a "Holy Priesthood".[9]

Baptists:

Our doctrine of the church determines our doctrine of the ministry. We hold firmly to the Priesthood of all Believers, and we have no separated order of priests. The ministry is for us a gift of the Spirit and the church, and is an office involving both an inward call of God and the commission of the church. We can discover no ground for believing that such a commission can be given only through an episcopate, and we hold that the individual church is competent and confer it. For us there is no more exalted office than a ministry charged with the preaching of the Word of God and with the care of souls. Yet any full description of the ministerial functions exercised among us must take account of other believers who, at the call of the Church, may preside at the observance of the Lord's Supper of fulfill any other duties which the church assigns to them.[10]

Puritans:

Thomas Cartwright says, "It is very true that all Christians are priests to offer up spiritual sacrifices; so are they all Kings to minister and overrule their evil concupiscences, which make rebellion against good notions of God's Spirit in men".[11]

Anglicans:

Book of Common Prayer
The English Bible meant that God was able to speak to individuals through the medium of His Word; the Prayer Book meant that individuals were able to come together as a corporate body so that they were no longer passive spectators of something that they did not understand, but active participants in the general confessions and thanksgivings of the church. The service of the church were now within the need of the laity, and the whole congregation was able to take part in the various acts of worship.[12]

There is some controversy among Anglicans as to when a Christian becomes a part of the Royal Priesthood. Some believe that this occurs at baptism, while others think after confirmation. C. Smyth believed, "If the Gospel is to be preached to every creature, it may, of necessity, having regard to the

conditions of the time, **be preached by any creature who has received it**, whether he be cleric or layman, or even laywomen for that matter, and whether he be within or without the Ecclesiastical establishment."[13]
Confessions of Faith:

In discussing his belief in the Priesthood of Believers, Charlie Shedd quotes chapter XXVIII, paragraph 1 of the Confessions of Faith:

> All saints being wanted to Jesus Christ their head, by His Spirit and by faith, here fellowship with Him in His grace, suffering, death, resurrection, and glory; and being wanted to one another in love, they have communion in each other's gifts and graces, and are obliged to the performances of such duties, public or private, or do conduce to their mutual good both in the inward and outward man.[14]

Roman Catholic:

The vast tradition of the Roman Catholic Church would take a monumental work to discuss. The views of two Roman Catholics will be shared to demonstrate an acceptance of universal priesthood by some.

James Coriden

Official ministers are not to perform the church's mission in place of the baptized, as substitutes or standins, rather they are to prepare and encourage, to help and urge the faithful to exercise their irreplaceable and crucial work in the world.[15]

Hans Kung

Certainly, there are very many modern theologians who are highly respected. One such theologian is Dr. Hans Kung, professor of theology at Tubingen University, Germany. His thoughts are worth looking at. In speaking about Hans Kung, Oscar Feucht states, "Throughout his timely book this biblical theologian calls for a return to the New Testament concept of the church, not as a highly organized institution but as a minister of **all believers** witnessing to Christ in every walk and station in life. It is significant that his book carries the subtitle: 'A Proposal for a New Church Ministry'."[16] New Testament ministry is capsuled by Kung with fives sentences:

(1) The church is above all else "the people of God," a community of believers.

(2) Ministry is a mutual service.

(3) The priesthood of all believers is clearly the New Testament pattern.

(4) The church is nurtured by means of the Word and sharing of the charismatic gifts.

(5) Everywhere it is the local church that is to be recognized.[17]

Independent Christian Church:

The premise of this body of believers has its roots in the Restoration Movement which was influenced by the Reformation. Alexander Campbell, one of this movement's primary endorsers, strongly denounced the "Hireling Clergy" during the American Frontier days. Campbell believed Protestantism, in some respects, had strayed from the New Testament concept of a universal priesthood. He deeply believed in this premise and developed it into a central teaching of this movement.[18]

NOTES

[1]Eastwood, *Priesthood of Believers*, pp. 34, 35, 40.
[2]*Ibid.*, p. 13.
[3]Getz, *The Measure of a Church*,
[4]Feucht, *Everyone a Minister*, p. 39.
[5]Eastwood, *Priesthood of Believers*, p. 133.
[6]*Idem, Royal Priesthood*, pp. 46-50.
[7]Idem, *Priesthood of Believers*, pp. 1, 60.
[8]Eastwood, *Priesthood of Believers*, p. 90.
[9]J. March, *Ways of Worship Report* (1951), p. 156.
[10]Alfred Underwood, *A History of English Baptists* (London: Carey Kingsgate Press, 1947), p. 262.
[11]Eastwood, *Priesthood of Believers*, p. 133.
[12]*Ibid.*, p.99.

[13]Charles Smyth, *Charles Simeon and Church Order* (Cambridge, England: University Press, 1940), p. 265.

[14]Charles Shedd, *The Pastoral Ministry of Church Officers*, p. 15.

[15]James Coriden, "Future Ministries in the Church," *Origins* 4 (December 19, 1974): 26:404.

[16]Feucht, *Everyone a Minister*, p. 15.

[17]Kung, *Why Priests?*, p. 58.

[18]Benjamin, *The Growing Congregation*, pp. 26, 27.

NOTES ON THE ROLE OF THE PASTOR

Jay Adams in *Pastoral Leadership* on pages 25-26 states, "When a pastor on his own tries to do the work of an entire congregation,

(1) He fails because he does not have the blessing of Christ upon his program; he has substituted (well meaningly, perhaps, but not-the-less highhandedly substituted) a human plan for the divine one.

(2) He fails because he does not have the many opportunities and contact that only the members of his congregation have.

(3) He fails because he spreads himself too thin, trying to do too much as one person. It is nothing less than pride for any one individual think that he is capable of doing what God has said is the work of an entire congregation.

(4) He fails also as a pastor-teacher. In spreading himself so thinly over the works of evangelism as well as that of shepherding and of teaching, he does none of these things well. His sermons suffer, his members are not cared for and even the fruit of the evangelism usually is minimal.

(5) He fails and this is the most significant failure of all because, wittingly or unwittingly, he has disobeyed and thereby dishonored the Chief Shepherd by whom he had "given" to the church in order to shepherd and teach so that the sheep might discover, develop and deploy their own gifts. Thus he failed to equip each member for his own "work" of the ministry of evangelism, which in part, belongs to every member.

A SHEPHERDING PROGRAM IN THE LOCAL CHURCH
Joe Grana
Central Christian Church
Beloit, Wisconsin

Definition: Shepherding is the active care by the church of her members. It is the functioning of that purpose of the church which nurtures people in Christ.

I. The Theological Rationale

There are many Scriptures which depict the need of Shepherding in the church. Here are a few:

John 10:11-18	"I am the Good Shepherd." (We are to follow Jesus' example.)
John 21:15-19	"Jesus said to Peter, "Feed my sheep!"
Acts 20:17-35	Eldership seen as pastoring the flock.
I Peter 2:4-10	"But you are a Royal Priesthood."
Galatians 6:2	"Bear one another's burdens."
James 5:16	"Confess your sins to one another."

Galatians 6:10	"Do good unto all men, but especially unto those of the household of faith."
Ephesians 2:19-22	"You are fellow citizens and members of the household of God."
James 1:27	"Religion pure and undefiled . . . to visit orphans and widows in their afflictions."
Romans 12:13	"Contribute to the needs of the Saints, practice hospitality."
Romans 12:15	"Rejoice with those who rejoice, weep with those who weep."
Galatians 6:1	"If any man is overtaken in any trespass, you who are spiritual should restore him in a spirit of gentleness."
John 13:34	"Love one another."
Matthew 7:12	"Do unto others as you would have them do unto you."
Acts 2:42f	"And they devoted themselves to . . . fellowship."

As seen in these verses, Shepherding is care which results in healing, sustaining, and guiding.

II. The Need for Shepherding
  A. Cultural Trends
     1. Lack of community concern and high degree of individualism.
     2. Specialization often causing fragmentation and isolation. (Christianity cuts through these barriers.)
  B. Individual Church Needs
     1. Size of a church
        a. As the church grows people are often lost in the crowd. Isolation is more common.
        b. The job is more than one man (pastor) or a small group of people (elders) can handle.
     2. Fragmentation
        a. Members coming from several communities (Beloit includes six towns.)
        b. Past history of church split.
     3. People desire personal (or small group) care and attention.
III. Job Description
  (See Appendix II)
IV. Organization of Shepherd Program
  A. Mainly geographical: shepherd from area too (if possible).
  B. Present Organization
     1. Presently we have thirty-seven (37) shepherds with six (6) to eight (8) families. Shepherds can be men, women, or couples.
     2. This number of families seems to be all one shepherd can adequately and comfortably handle. If there are enough

109

shepherds to handle as few as four families, all the better.

3. Families include members (if one person in family is member whole family is cared for unless they refuse) and regularly attending non-members.

C. Supervision

1. Shepherds meet bi-monthly to share concerns.

2. Each shepherd is assigned to an Elder for his individual oversight.

D. Listings

1. Alphabetically by families. (Fictitious names)

	Shepherd
Acker, Louis	Carol Smith
Aimer, Margy	Tom Williams
Alexander, Fred	John Doe
Alexander, Sally	John Doe
Apple, Red	Bob Kind

2. According to Shepherd

(1) **Dick Dill**	(2) **Charlotte Homer**
John Brown	Dean Bart
Ken Hart	Thomas Dark
Tom Hazelt	Joe Grand
Sue Jacobs	Vern Hurl
Bill Kool	Tim Hanson
Art Pen	George Littel
Joe Stool	

V. Securing Shepherds

A. Explain program and ask for volunteers

1. In newsletter and bulletin

2. From pulpit

B. Talk to specific individuals

1. Suggested by elders or committee

2. As a result of talent survey or questionnaire

VI. Training Shepherds
   A. This is a very vital part of the program. People feel a little more secure about serving if they know they are being helped to become more competent. For 1977 our group had planned three training sessions with the following focus:
      1. Leadership development
      2. Gift development (Spirit-filled life)
      3. Communication and Sensitivity
   B. Training to some degree takes place with each shepherd personally and during the bi-monthly meetings.
VII. Evaluation of Shepherding Program
   A. Bi-monthly shepherd meeting
   B. Questionnaire given to congregation (intentionally kept short and simple)
   C. Opinions from people outside the local congregation
   D. Take an at random telephone survey of "fringe-area" members
      1. Has your shepherd contacted you?
      2. Has the shepherd program made any difference to you?
      3. What do you think of the Shepherding Program?
VIII. A. Become a sharing group
   B. Conduct home Bible studies
   C. Have monthly fellowship meals
   D. Do calling on church visitors for the area
   E. Become an evangelistic arm of the church

SHEPHERD JOB DESCRIPTION
Central Christian Church
Beloit, Wisconsin

1. Maintain personal touch every six to eight weeks.
2. Visit in case of sickness or death.
3. Help find areas of service.
4. Act as telephone committee.
5. Assist in distributing sheets.
6. Offer one's services.

(1) Personal Contact

Contact is defined as "talking to the person." This can be done in a face to face encounter or on the telephone. Contacts could be made at church, casually on the street or at stores, during special church or community activities, or due to special calls such as sickness, death, or extended absenteeism. The important factor is to let people know they are being thought about and cared for. One of the above contacts is to be made every six to eight weeks.

(2) Sickness

Upon finding out about sickness, (usually the church office will call) send a card immediately. The minister or church office will advise whether a visit is appropriate or not. This fact is considered because some people do not desire visitors while others may not be able to welcome visitors (intensive care, isolation). If the person cannot be seen, it is suggested that a family member be contacted to relay concern and to see how the church can minister to the family. If at all possible, the shepherd should visit or phone a hospital patient.

In case of death in the family the Shepherd will

make a personal visit at the individual's home, visitation, or funeral service. A sympathy card should also be sent.

(3) Areas of Service

Frequently, members of the church relay to each other areas of service, but do not tell the minister or elders. The Shepherd can assist greatly in this area by passing the word along to the elders or minister. Furthermore, as the Shepherd grows in his relationship with his people, he may see that the person has abilities or interests which could be used in the church. This information can also be passed along, for the elders may not know of these abilities or interests and have not considered the person for some particular service.

(4) Telephone Committee

The Shepherding Program is a built-in network of communication for the congregation. Telephoning the complete congregation may be necessary in cases of special prayers, congregational business meetings, revival services, or appointments for such things as a church directory. By having the shepherds call, it is possible to contact the whole congregation in a short period of time without placing too heavy a burden on anyone.

(5) Questionnaire Distribution

At times the church surveys congregational talent and interest, evaluations of various programs of the congregation, or other written responses. It has been found that the congregation participates more fully when personally confronted with these sheets than just simply placing them in the church paper or bulletin. The Shepherd's responsibility would be to get the sheets to his people and pick them up (or make other arrangements) from them. This process allows opportunity for a reason to make a contact.

(6) Offering Services

Shepherds are to communicate their availability to help the person when in need. Some Shepherds have given these people rides to the doctor, helped fix cars, baked pies, etc. It is suggested that each family have the Shepherd's name, address, and telephone number.

(7) People Responsible For

Each Shepherd is responsible for the care of six to eight families. These families either have at least one person who is a member of the church or the family has been attending regularly for about three months. The list one has may change due to additions of new members, deletions from having moved away, or death, or exchanging with a different Shepherd for personal reasons. This will only be done when necessary and with the consent of the elders and minister.

(8) Chain of Responsibility

Ultimately every Christian is responsible to God. The Shepherding Program is not tightly or strictly controlled, but each Shepherd will be assigned to an elder who will oversee his work. The minister will also work with each Shepherd.

(9) Term

The time of service is one year beginning September 1 of each year. At this time a Shepherd may continue, terminate his service, or exchange lists with another Shepherd.

(10) Training

Through the course of each year there will be approximately three seminars with Shepherds in mind. If at all possible, it is hoped that each Shepherd will attend these training sessions to increase his capacity for ministry. The elders and minister are also always available for consultation.

ACTIVE LISTENING EXERCISE

A. TELLER GUIDELINES

Task: to present a need, issue, opportunity or problem so your listener fully understands it.

1. Ask for a measure of understanding from the listener.
2. Initiate illustrations and examples as appropriate.
3. Provide correct definitions, not assuming common agreement on terms.
4. Keep discourse on track.

B. LISTENER GUIDELINES

Task: to help the teller tell his tale.

1. Do not introduce new ideas of your own.
2. Restate what you have heard: paraphrase.
3. As for confirmation as to whether you heard correctly.
4. Ask for examples or illustrations for expansion of ideas.
5. Ask for definitions where appropriate.

Human Relations:
Community Meeting

Schutz distinguishes three interpersonal need areas: (1) inclusion, (2) control and (3) affection. This lab will deal only with inclusion. Schutz defines inclusion as the need to be associated with people, to belong. It is manifested as wanting to be attended to, and to attract attention and interest.

Essential aspect of inclusion: People want to be included as distinct persons who have identity and as individuals worthy of being understood.

Too little inclusion: The undersocial seeks isolation. He tends to be withdrawn and introverted. Unconsciously, he wants others to pay attention to him. Privately he feels others don't understand him. Because people don't consider him, he feels worthless.

Successful resolution of inclusion in childhood: For this person interaction is no problem. He is comfortable with people or alone. He is capable of strong commitment with groups or can withhold commitment if he wishes to. Unconsciously, he feels worthwhile and significant.

Maslow says:
"If both the physiological and the safety needs are fairly well gratified, there will emerge the love and affection and belongingness needs. The person will hunger for affectionate relations with people in general, namely, for a place in his group, and he will strive with great intensity to achieve this goal.

In our society the thwarting of the belongingness and love needs is the most commonly found core in cases of maladjustment and more sever psychopathology."

116

Human Relations:
Dyadic Exchange:
Select one of the following, fill in the blank, then exchange with your dyadic partner:

   1.   I feel excluded at home/school/work when . . .

   2.   I can't stand being alone. I seek people constantly because . . .

   3.   When I see a group, I don't wait for anyone to invite me in; I walk in and feel comfortable because I know that . . .

Whipping around:
   You might tell the group whether your predominant trait is to be undersocial, oversocial or comfortable with people as well as alone.

Human Relations: "Are you empathic?"

Community Meeting:

In the previous lab, we worked in areas of control. We probed our behavioral pattern to see whether we are generally too low, high or balanced in our interpersonal need for control. How much responsibility do we presently assume? Today, we will look into our need for affection; then we will consider various aspects of empathic behavior that make for warm and genuine communication. The input is from Shutz, Carol Dye, Erich Fromm and Marshall Rosenberg. Shutz says:

> Affection behavior refers to close personal emotional feelings between two people. The effort is to avoid being engulfed in emotional entanglement (not being free to relate without a deep involvement), but also to avoid having too little affection and a bleak, sterile life without love, warmth, tenderness, and someone to confide in.

Too Little Affection:

The underpersonal type tends to avoid close and personal ties with others. He maintains his two-person relations on a superficial, distant level and is most uncomfortable when others do the same with him. Unconsciously, he seeks a satisfactory affectional relation. His fear is that no one loves him. In a group situation he is afraid he won't be liked. Either he rejects and avoids people or he is superficially friendly to everyone. He believes he is unlovable and doesn't want others to discover it.

Too Much Affection:

The overpersonal type attempts to become extremely close to others. He wants others to treat him in a very close, personal way. His unconscious feeling is, "My first experiences with affection were painful, but personal. If I try again, they will be better." The affection anxiety is that the self is nasty and unlovable.

Successful resolution of affection in childhood:
For this person emotional relations are no problem.
He feels comfortable in personal relations as well as in
a situation requiring emotional distance. He feels that
he is a lovable person, and that he is capable of
genuine affection.

Comparison: The inclusion anxiety . . . the self is
worthless, empty. The control anxiety . . . the self is
irresponsible. The affection anxiety . . . the self is
unlovable, nasty. Inclusion is concerned with the
problem of in or out. Control is concerned with top or
bottom. Affection is concerned with close or far.

Human Relations: "Are you empathic?"

Dyadic exchange:

Complete the following, then exchange with your
dyadic partner.
1. Are you generally underpersonal, avoiding close
    and personal relationships: **Specific example:**

2. Are you generally overpersonal, attempting to
    become extremely close to others? **Specific
    example:**

3. Do you feel comfortable in personal relations as
    well as in situations requiring emotional distance?
    Specific example:

	SOME		
NEVER	TIMES	USUALLY	ALWAYS

.... 1. Are you interested in other people?

.... 2. Do you make friends of both sexes?

.... 3. Do you make friends with young children and older people as well as with people your own age?

.... 4. Do you admit that you are sometimes wrong?

.... 5. Do you control your temper?

.... 6. Do you try to see the other person's point of view?

.... 7. Do you listen while others are talking?

.... 8. Do you try to keep worries and problems to yourself without airing them to everyone you meet?

.... 9. Are you dependable?

.... 10. Are you willing to follow as well as lead?

.... 11. Are you cheerful?

.... 12. Can you accept other's ideas?

.... 13. Are you honest with yourself?

....14. Do you have moody spells?

....15. Can you get over moody spells fairly quickly?

....16. Do you complain about your aches and pains?

....17. Can you take teasing as well as give it?

....18. Do you maintain a balance between work and play?

....19. Do you profit by past experiences?

....20. Do you refrain from gossip?

....21. Do you find fault with   others needlessly?

....22. Do you keep your promises?

....23. Are you well-mannered?

....24. Are you on time for appointments?

....25. Do you get along well with yourself?

Think about your answers to these questions in preparation for the group discussion that follows.
Other exercises are available upon request. These exercises assist shepherds in communication skills.

APPENDIX IV
SAMPLE LETTERS

Dear Shepherd,

Enclosed you will find the updated Shepherd lists and a job description. As you look at the lists you may find a change or two. This change has occured for the following reasons:

(1) No elder has a list
(2) Each elder is a Shepherd or overseer of a group of Shepherds.
(3) Therefore, if a fellow Shepherd was on your list, he is no more. He has been placed on an elder's list.

We hope that this change will help our program to work more smoothly. The elder's responsibility to the Shepherds is two-fold: (1) Shepherding them according to their needs. (2) Oversee them to make sure they are fulfilling their responsibilities as Shepherds.

This change has been made possible because seven (7) more people have agreed to be Shepherds. Praise the Lord.

I am presently planning a Shepherd's meeting for Wednesday, October 5 at 8:00 p.m. Please plan now to be there.

Thank you for your willingness to work. May the Lord richly bless you in your ministry.

In Christ's Service

Joe Grana

Dear Shepherd,

At our last meeting we decided two significant matters. (1) Because we were six (6) Shepherds short it would be most helpful to have all the present Shepherds increase their list to eight (8). In this manner everyone in the congregation would presently be covered. As agreed in the job description you will never have more than eight (8). Therefore, your list may be increased. Please check that and contact those people.

(2) We decided to evaluate our program: therefore, for those of you who were not at the meeting, there is enclosed the evaluation sheet to be filled out by your families on your list. Please return these to me by May 1st.

The purpose of this is two-fold: (1) To help improve the program according to the needs of the congregation. (2) To assist me in writing of my disquisition about the Shepherding program.

Thank you for your dedicated work. If you need any help please feel free to contact me or the elder who is your Shepherd.

May the Lord richly bless your ministry and may you find satisfaction in it.

In His Service,

Joe Grana

BIBLIOGRAPHY

Adams, Jay. *Pastoral Leadership.* Grand Rapids: Baker Book House, 1975.

Adams, Jay. *The Pastoral Life.* Grand Rapids: Baker Book House, 1974.

Benjamin, Paul. *The Growing Congregation.* Lincoln, Illinois: Lincoln Christian College Press, 1972.

Beyerhaus, Peter. *Missions: Which Way?* Grand Rapids: Zondervan, 1971.

Biersdorf, John, ed. *Creating an Intentional Ministry.* Nashville: Abingdon, 1976.

Calian, Carnegie Samuel. *Today's Pastor in Tomorrow's World.* New York: Hawthorn Books, 1977.

Cox, Harvey. *The Secular City.* New York: Macmillan, 1965.

Drucker, Peter. *Management.* New York: Harper & Row, 1974.

Dulles, Avery. *Models of the Church.* Garden City, New York: Doubleday, 1974.

Eastwood, Cyril. *The Priesthood of all Believers.* Minneapolis: Augsburg Publishing House, 1963.

Eastwood, Cyril. *The Royal Priesthood of the Faithful.* Minneapolis: Augsburg Publishing House, 1963.

Edge, Finley. *The Greening of the Church.* Waco, Texas: Word Books, 1971.

Feucht, Oscar. *Everyone a Minister.* St. Louis: Concordia Publishing House, 1974.

Getz, Gene. *The Measure of a Church.* Glendale, California: Regal Books, 1975.

Gibbs, Mark and Morton, T. Ralph. *God's Frozen People.* Philadelphia: Westminster Press, 1964.

Girard, Robert. *Brethren, Hang Loose.* Grand Rapids: Zondervan, 1972.

Greenslade, S. L. *Shepherding the Flock.* Naperville, Illinois: SCM Book Club, 1967.

Hiltner, Seward. *The Christian Shepherd.* New York: Abingdon Press, 1959.

Hiltner, Seward. *Ferment in the Ministry.* New York: Abingdon Press, 1969.

Hodges, Melvin. *The Indigenous Church.* Springfield, Missouri: David McKay Co., 1953.

Holland, Cornelius Joseph. *The Shepherd and His Flock.* New York: David McKay Co., 1953.

Kittel, Gerhard. *Theological Dictionary of the New Testament.* (Vol. 3) Grand Rapids: Eerdman Publishing Co., 1965.

125

Kung, Hans. *Why Priests? A Proposal for a New Church Ministry.* Garden City, New York: Doubleday, 1972.

MacNutt, Francis o.p. *Healing.* Notre Dame, Indiana: Ave Marie Press, 1974.

March, J. *Ways of Worship Report.* 1951.

Moulton, W. F. and Geden, A. S. *A Concordance to the Greek Testament.* Edinburgh: T. & T. Clark, 1950.

Pusey, Nathan and Taylor, Charles. *Ministry for Tomorrow.* New York: Seabury Press, 1967.

Qualben, Lars. *A History of the Christian Church.* New York: Thomas Nelson & Sons, 1950.

Richards, Larry. *Regions Beyond.* Fullerton, California: David C. Cook Publishing Co., 1977.

Schaefer, Francis. *The Church at the End of the 20th Century.* Downers Grove, Illinois: Inter-Varsity Press, 1970.

Schaller, Lyle. *The Decision-Makers.* Nashville: Abingdon, 1974.

Schaller, Lyle. *The Pastor and the People.* Nashville: Abingdon, 1973.

Shedd, Charles. *The Pastoral Ministry of Church Officers.* Atlanta: John Knox Press, 1977.

Smyth, Charles. *Charles Simeon and Church Order.* Cambridge, England: University Press, 1940.

Snaith, Norman. *The Distinctive Ideas of the Old Testament.* London: Epworth Press, 1944.

Southard, Samuel. *Comprehensive Pastoral Care.* Valley Forge: Judson Press, 1975.

Stedman, Ray. *Body Life.* Glendale, California: Regal Books, 1972.

Stowe, Eugene. *The Ministry of Shepherding.* Kansas City, Missouri: Beacon Hill Press, 1976.

Trueblood, Elton. *The Incendiary Fellowship.* New York: Harper & Row, 1967.

Ullestad, Norman. "The Priesthood of Believers Plans for Tomorrow." D. Min. Disquisition, Wartburg Theological Seminary, 1976.

Underwood, Alfred. *A History of the English Baptists.* London: Carey Kingsgate Press, 1947.

Vine, W. E. *An Expository Dictionary of New Testament Words.* (Vol. 1-4) Old Tappan, New Jersey: Fleming Revell Co., 1966.

PERIODICALS

Best, E. "I Peter 2:4-10: A Reconsideration." *Novum Testamentum* 4 (1969): 270-93.

Best, E. "Spiritual Sacrifices in General Priesthood in the New Testament." *Interpretation* 14 (July 1960): 18-31.

Coriden, James. "Future Ministries in the Church." *Origins* 4 (December 19, 1974): 401-10.

Elliot, John. "Death of a Slogan: From Royal Priests to Celebrating Community." *Una Sancta* 25 (1968): 3: 18-31.

Francis, Martin. "Image of Shepherd in the Gospel of St. Matthew." *Science Et Esprit* 27 (October-December 1975): 261-301.

Hairston, Andrew. "The Kingdom meets Human Needs." *Christian Standard* (March 28, 1976): 5-7.

Knight, J. A. "Psychiatrist in the Life and Work of the Church." *Pastoral Psychology* 15 (December 1964): 6-12.

Littell, Franklin. "The Ministry of the Laity." *Pastoral Psychology* 15 (December 1964): 6-12.

Lown, W. F. "On Feeding Sheep." *Christian Standard* (April 18, 1976): 13.

McBain, L. D. "Clergy-Lay Issues and Relations: The Baptist Perspective." *Foundations* 15 (April-June 1972): 156-62.

Nash, Donald. "Clergy." *Voice of Kentucky Christian College* 20 (October 1977): 3:

Von Saver, Rohr A. "Fact and Image in the Shepherd Psalm." *Concordia Theological Monthly* 42 (September 1971): 488-92.

Schaeffer, Edith. "Hospitality: Optional or Commanded?" *Christian Standard* (December 17, 1976): 28-9.

Wright, Jo Robert. "Canterbury Statement and the Five Priesthoods." *Anglican Theological Review* 57 (October 1975): 446-56.